CRAFT GALLERIES

A Directory of English Galleries
and their Craftspeople

Edited by Caroline Mornement

TONY WILLIAMS PUBLICATIONS

Published in Great Britain by Tony Williams Publications
24a Queen Square, North Curry, Taunton, Somerset TA3 6LE

Typesetting by Interface 0395 68681
Printed and bound in Great Britain by J H Haynes & Co. Ltd.
Sparkford, Somerset

Trade Sales: Derek Searle Associates 0753 539295
Distribution: Little Red Witch Books 0823 490080

All other sales enquiries should be referred to Little Red Witch Books,
or the editor, Caroline Mornement 0935 862731

ISBN 1 869833 45 7

EDITOR'S VIEW

Compiling this Directory has been a varied experience. It has been:

Encouraging to see the enthusiasm with which the participating gallery owners have tackled the task of collecting together a group of craftspeople of their choice.

Interesting to open the packages of texts and photographs sent in by craftspeople, and to see such a wide range of good quality crafts.

Intriguing to have conversations with so many gallery owners and craftspeople; to receive their encouragement and views on this venture and to be continually amazed at the varied range of talents that exist.

Inspiring to look forward to the next edition, when I hope that there will be a wider choice of galleries taking part

It was felt sensible to start this Directory on a small scale; contacts were made to only a limited number of galleries. For subsequent editions it is proposed to cover a wider area, more intensively.

Therefore the publishers and I sincerely hope that this will be the first of many Craft Galleries Directories. I'm sure that the first edition of the "Cricketers' Wisden" or "Rothmans' Football Year Book" were much smaller than they are today!

Caroline Mornement

Anyone interested in contributing to the next edition should contact Caroline Mornement via Alpha Gallery.

PARNHAM

- ❖ home of John Makepeace and his furniture workshops

- ❖ also of Parnham College — for designers and craftsmen in wood

- ❖ that rare occurrence in Britain — an historic house dedicated to a professional practice, education, and the promotion of contemporary applied arts, paintings and sculpture

- ❖ and, nearby, Hooke Park College, researching, demonstrating and teaching the disciplines of design, industrial production and business development through training and commercial experience in the use of indigenous and renewable forest resources

Photo: George Wright

The House and Gardens, the John Makepeace Furniture Workshop, and Hooke Park College are open to visitors from 10.00 am to 5.00 pm each Sunday, Wednesday and Bank Holiday from April to October inclusive.

Parnham House, Beaminster, Dorset DT8 3NA
Telephone 0308 862204 Fax 0308 863494

INTRODUCTION

One of the most rewarding discoveries in my early years was the realisation that everything is connected — that cause and result are part of a continuum. The way education, our working lives and Government tend to be packaged fosters discrete areas of knowledge and understanding, with actions being constrained accordingly. But artists and makers of objects can respond to a boundless range of nature and knowledge.

Recognising the wholeness of nature and the inevitability of relationships between form and function, in nature as in objects, is part of the artist's currency. Awareness of the changing context liberates us from tradition, whilst stimulating a deeper understanding of the rôle of art as an expression of individual values of significance. The extraordinary liberties enjoyed by artists bring with them the call for personal and public accountability.

Nature provides our materials. Man removes and reshapes them — with, or without, knowledge and conscience.

Just as leading companies are increasingly concerned to conserve

Triad Table. Yew

the natural environment, artists and makers have an important part to play in reconciling conflicts and giving cogent expression to their solutions through their work. Art is about our own time, whilst pointing the way to the future.

The publishers of this Directory are clearly looking to the future and the encouragement of the enormous potential among young people now launching their careers, for whom galleries play such an important rôle. Every success to them and to this splendid initiative.

John Makepeace
Parnham House

ALPHA GALLERY

51 Winchester Street, Salisbury, Wiltshire SP1 1HL (0722) 414122

Open Tuesday to Saturday 10am - 4.30pm throughout the year

I n 1984, with my youngest child at school, I had time to concentrate on a home based project. Having trained as an interior designer, I had already been painting furniture for pin money, and now needed an outlet from which to sell, so the idea of Alpha was formed.

With a friend in a similar situation, we set to work to 'do up' three derelict stables in the grounds of our old farmhouse in East Coker, from which to run an arts and crafts gallery.

We enjoyed the challenge, husbands helped, and Alpha opened in May 1984. We soon realised why it was necessary to have changing exhibitions and tentatively began a programme, showing work mainly by local artists at this stage. The partner/friend moved away after the first year, but as I was enjoying hunting out good quality unusual

crafts, I continued. The gallery became established and put on some very successful painting exhibitions, showing work by Ron Jesty, Sheila Sanford and Sir Hugh Casson, among others.

However, a small country village, off the main road, is not the best situation and now that I had a good 'stable' of artists, it seemed time to move to a more populated area. After much thought and research, on foot, looking around local towns and their galleries, I settled on Salisbury. It was in the right direction i.e. towards London, and although well catered for with top of the market art, I felt that there was a gap in the middle range, and certainly nobody showing a wide selection of British craft.

Eventually a suitable property became vacant and in September 1989 Alpha opened in Winchester Street, Salisbury. It has gradually built up a following in this area; now many regulars pop into the two low-beamed rooms which lend themselves well to displaying the wide range of ceramics and wood which we show. The rear room has comfortable wall spaces for smaller paintings and etchings and the gallery continues to show small unusual exhibitions at regular intervals.

All correspondence to:
Burton Cottage Farm, East Coker, Yeovil, Somerset, BA 22 9LS Telephone 0935 86 2731

Caroline Mornement

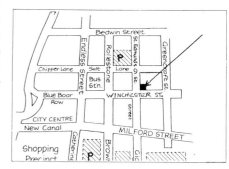

SUE FORD

People who know Sue Ford will tell you that it is no coincidence that she is heavily into mad March hares. After all, how many women give up a nice quiet domestic life and disappear off to art college at 44? Sue not only did just that but emerged three years later a lot more enlightened and with a hard-earned degree. Sue specialised in ceramics as it combined her love of modelling and the human and animal form.

Carrying her tradition of doing things the wrong way round, her first commission was for Knoll Gardens near Wimborne in Dorset, for whom she designed a large fountain/sculpture as part of a new formal garden. Her work since then has been more modest but no less popular. People who are owners of her sculptures are very proud of them and many have become regular clients. Sue's work is primarily for the garden and the greatest pleasure for her is to design pieces for individual gardens where the sculpture becomes an integral part of the landscape.

LAWSON E RUDGE

With special reference to the 'Flat Cow'

Many of the sculptures I make derive from my paintings, for example, the flat cow illustrated was a result of painting a landscape which was about the inter-relationship of cows, trees and clouds. I simply thought it would be an idea to make a cow on which to paint a landscape — hence the cow being flat — a kind of three-dimensional canvas.

Numbers, mainly two and five, feature frequently in my painting and sculpture, and for many years their meaning was a mystery even to me. However, I now think that their origins come from the days when I was a steam train spotter, a conclusion I came to when I compared a successful sculpture with a steam train. If one forgets the numerical values of two and five and views them in an abstract way, they can relate to the wheels of a steam engine, or to the movement of a swan, and more.

NICK REES

Woodfired Stoneware and Porcelain

A Nick Rees signed individual pot has exceptional rarity value. For, even though Nick has worked full-time for over 20 years at one of the country's leading studio potteries, the personal output of this unassuming Master Potter is extremely limited.

As a result, his work is especially appreciated by a growing number of collectors, who recognise it as being among the most skilled and aesthetically-sensitive produced today.

Born in Weston-super-Mare in 1949, Nick began a creative training course at Loughborough in 1967, which led to two years teaching in Coventry.

But in 1972, he changed direction to serve an apprenticeship with John Leach at Muchelney Pottery, Somerset, where he is now firmly established as Master Potter.

The continuing success of the Muchelney classic range owes much to Nick's deft hand, critical eye and skill in firing the large wood-fired kiln.

But, whilst he would be the first to agree that the work at Muchelney is challenging and fulfilling, nonetheless the urge for personal creative expression has grown in recent years.

About nine years ago, Nick began experimenting with form and texture in his spare time at his small home studio. Gradually, a distinctive personal Rees style has evolved — influenced without question by the Leach tradition, and increasingly by the shared experience of a 1984 study trip to Nigeria with John Leach.

Nick's pots, however, have a character very much their own; freely expressed yet precise; rounded and softly coloured yet subtly segmented, flattened or carved to accentuate the form.

PAULINE ZELINSKI

I was born in London in 1948 and studied 3-D Design, specialising in Ceramics at West Surrey College of Art and Design in Farnham. Initially, time was divided between teaching at Art Colleges and producing my own ceramics, taking part in exhibitions at home and abroad.

Working from my workshop in Exeter I have recently started using a white earthenware clay body to make large platters, dishes, bowls and pedestal bowls. The platters offer a good surface for me to paint onto, using underglaze colours. I enjoy mixing colours and the endless possibilities of colour combinations which can be used to produce patterns and paintings, the sources of which come predominantly from nature. The bowls and pedestal dishes also provide good shapes for decorating with a subtle build-up of tones and colour.

After being biscuit-fired, the pieces are then glazed with a transparent earthenware glaze which brings out the full brilliance of the colours underneath.

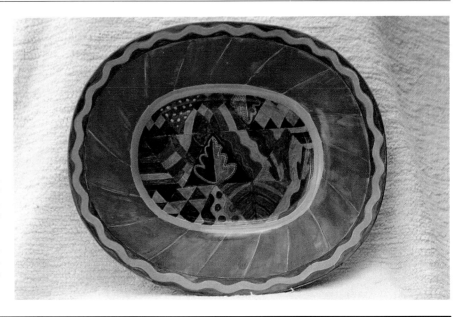

THE MEWS POTTERY

The Mews Pottery was started by Margot Moore, who studied art in Austria and Germany but turned to pottery after moving to Cheltenham.

From the beginning Margot decorated her thrown pots with small figures of people or animals. These figures, together with the handbuilt furniture, soon took over the whole capacity of the pottery.

Everything is made in high-fired stoneware or porcelain, using the traditional potters' skills and natural materials to impart to each piece a certain irregularity and quality all of its own, which means that no two pieces are ever the same. The tiny vases, pots and plates are all thrown on the wheel and hand decorated.

Musicians, first in stoneware but later in porcelain, have become collector's items around the world. Hot air balloons in white porcelain with bright on-glaze decoration are a more recent success.

Margot is now producing more and more one-off pieces and special commissions which are finding their way into many collections.

RICHARD WINDLEY

Starting a workshop to design and make in wood around 1976, I quickly became interested in the human impulse to hoard and secrete personal precious objects. This led to a long and slowly evolving series of small and intricate articulated boxes and containers which have been sold and exhibited in many British galleries over the years.

These boxes I continue to make and show, but recently a desire to work in a larger and freer way, combined with a particular affinity for strong, repetitive, rhythmic elements, has led to the development of a new series of large open bowls which are segmented and riveted in a deceptively simple way. This method of construction shows the character of the timber to dramatic effect and the forms seem to invoke complex resonances in the viewer — hints of fossils, insects, archaic boats, armour, marine animals and more.

HANNAH WHITWORTH

Sheepware

Born in 1953 in Greenwich, Hannah graduated from Bath Academy of Art, where she studied Three-dimensional Design, in the mid-seventies. Finding herself alienated from the prevailing studio stoneware derived from Far-Eastern traditions, she was drawn increasingly to the work of the peasant cultures of Europe, instantly attracted by their warmth, colour and humour.

Setting up in a workshop in Bath in 1979, Hannah began making commemorative pieces for individual customers, enjoying the tradition of personalising each piece using decoration predominantly derived from folk traditions.

These dictated working with earthenware clay bodies and temperatures and, most importantly, with slips — liquid clays — to achieve the characteristic decorative surfaces.

During the 1980s Hannah developed her tableware range, Sheepware, later refined in collaboration with more versatile throwers, notably Les Sharpe and Andrew Eddleston.

Slowly, as others moved on and demand for 'Sheepware' increased, Hannah took over the whole workshop premises, and now sells her tableware to galleries throughout the country.

The ware is thrown in a smooth terracotta clay and, when leather-hard, coated with a background of coloured slips. After further drying time the decorative creatures are applied in thicker slips, trailed onto the surface. After careful finishing, each piece is left to dry completely, given its preliminary 'biscuit' firing, then coated in a transparent glossy glaze and refired to 1125°C.

Presently raising her two small children as well as running the pottery, Hannah is looking forward to further developing work on large dishes and more individual pieces.

Photo: Lesley Billingham

SYLVIA ANTONSEN

Born in Bournemouth 1937, I trained as a painter at Bournemouth College of Art, moved to London in the early sixties and worked as a teacher, later combining this with bringing up a family. My own work output was limited during that time, although by 1985 I was able to carry out a number of portrait commissions, principally of children and animals. These last included a number of cat companion pieces using acrylics on plywood. It was the pleasure of painting on wood that led to the painted boxes.

A move to Bath in 1991 gave me the much talked about opportunity to 'give up teaching' and concentrate on painting. Starting points for the boxes can vary considerably, from a client's interests and the proposed contents of the drawers to objects that attract me like the juggling balls on the illustrated box.

ARTEMIDORUS

27b Half Moon Lane, Herne Hill, London SE24 9JU. Telephone 071 737 7747

Open Tuesday to Friday 10.30am - 7pm, Saturday 10am-6pm, Sunday/Monday throughout December

Artemidorus, run by Amanda Walbank, is in Herne Hill. Set back slightly where the shops end and before the houses start, its singularity catches the eye. Narrow, suggesting perhaps a chapel, it appears Victorian, but was built in 1989.

The interior, one room upstairs and one down, has been renovated by John Bell, her husband, a designer. It shows how much can be achieved by a sensitive response to the original qualities of a building. Though one never forgets the slimness of the rooms, which is part of their appeal, there is a sense of lightness and space — allowing Amanda the opportunity to exercise her instinct for decorative artefacts. You enter a space filled with colour. Deeply coloured glassware, brightly painted toys, richly glazed ceramics, hand painted silks, amidst cool white walls. Virtually everything is hand crafted and very inviting to hold.

A saleable price, quality craftsmanship and Amanda's taste are the factors that determine the contents. The range of stock is unexpected; there are children's toys and books, knitwear, T-shirts, stationery, glasses, beakers, vases; there are jugs and bowls, jewellery and metalwork; mirrors, clocks, ties and scarves; things made of wood exploiting natural grains; the sort of cards and wrap you find only occasionally outside central London; and blue bottles of cosmetics and essential oils (the place is aromatic too) that capture the other lights in the shop. There is an evident flair for choosing and setting things off against each other. It is clearly a place that people like to enter and browse, as well as buy in.

The main Gallery space is upstairs and exhibitions change every six to eight weeks. Younger artists are favoured, but more established artists such as the abstract

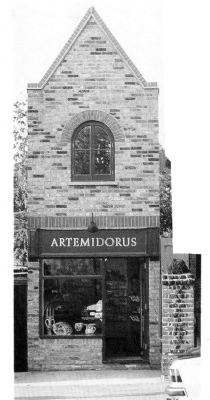

landscapist Bé van der Heide and the architectural engraver Alison Neville are also shown. This is the same policy that operates in the shop where, for example, glass by Anthony Stern, jewellery by Sophie Harley or Peter Chatwin and Pamela Martin can be found alongside the work of craftspeople as yet relatively unknown. The artworks have a strong decorative element — they avoid all cosiness and portray a comic perspective on the world. There have been exhibitions of etchings, water colours, textile works, paper works and print works. Three dimensional works such as ceramics by Jitka Palmer, wooden vessels by Philip Harfield and metalwork by Richard Pell often complement the space. A small collection of original prints and other works from previous exhibitions are usually kept in stock.

Founded in the midst of recession and celebrating their first year, the reputation of Artemidorus and The Gallery continues to grow and the auguries seem good. Artemidorus, incidentally, was a Greek philosopher and soothsayer who offered 'the interpretaion of dreams' — in some way the name is not misplaced.

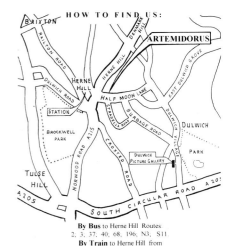

HOW TO FIND US:

By Bus to Herne Hill. Routes: 2; 3; 37; 40; 68; 196; N3; S11.
By Train to Herne Hill from Victoria (10 minutes), Blackfriars & Thameslink (12 minutes)
By Road or walking
Herne Hill is 4 miles South of the City of London. Trafalgar Square is 4 miles, Westminster 3 miles and *Dulwich Picture Gallery*, park and village is less than 1 mile East.

SOPHIE HARLEY
Jewellery Designer

Following graduation from her MA in Jewellery Design at the Royal College of Art, Sophie joined three other design students to form the New Renaissance; her jewellery providing a perfect foil for their original and witty outfits. The team's work has been exhibited widely; recently a specially designed dress (accessoried with Sophie's jewels) featured in the exclusive 'Court Couture 1992' exhibition at Kensington Palace, and they have just had their first exhibition in Tokyo.

Angelic baby seahorses, mediæval suns, stars and hearts all feature in Sophie's distinctive creations. She uses her considerable skill to produce exquisite pieces in etched oxidised silver, 24 carat gold leaf and acid-etched enamel. The range includes designs for men and women — discreet studs, flamboyant dangly ear-rings, covetable charm bracelets, graceful long necklaces, chunky rings, delightful brooches, nifty stick pins and stylish cufflinks.

Sophie also designs to clients' individual specifications and has created one-off pieces for Mappin & Webb's 'Celebration of Gold' and diamond ear-rings for De Beer's 'Diamond Showcase 1991'. One of her most notable and devoted clients is Enya, who has adopted Sophie's stunning designs as part of her signature look.

Photo: Kate Dumbleton

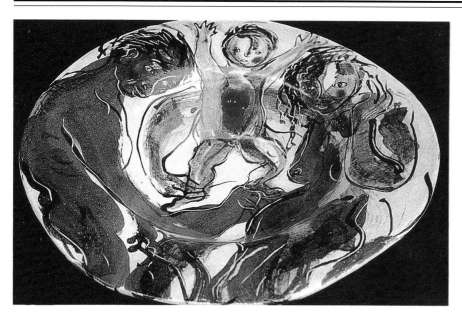

JITKA PALMER
Ceramics

Born in 1959, Jitka is from Czechoslovakia. Although she has been working with clay for over 12 years, her path has not been particularly straightforward or conventional. After qualifying as a doctor, she married an Englishman and settled in London. The transition led her to leave medicine and to further her study of ceramics at Croydon College of Art & Design. She later received a Crafts Council grant.

In Jitka's own words 'I make clay vessels and wrap them up in paintings. The paintings do not necessarily follow the shape of the vessel. I do not seek perfection. I make clay shapes my own way, like a sculpture. Then I paint 'the picture' using traditional glazes, slips, oxides and stains ... always figurative. It is people I am interested in, living people — imperfect, spontaneous, moving ... past, present and sometimes imaginary ... each piece is individual.'

The scope of Jitka's work is varied from large wall pieces and ceramic kites to more practical bowls, jugs and vases. Her work is expressive and alive.

RICHARD PELL
Creative Metalwork

Born in 1962, Richard studied Fine Art at Wimbledon College of Art and Middlesex Polytechnic. Whilst at college he specialised in sculpture created mainly from recycled metal and exploring the processes involved in developing mobile sculptures.

He has exhibited at many London venues including the Barbican and the ICA. His sculptural works display a distinct sense of humour that makes them very approachable. They vary considerably in size, from small coffee table pieces to a full-sized motorized crocodile tank, offering compartments for four people, carrying several machine guns and a mean set of teeth!

He has also established his own business, creating and making metal artefacts such as candelabra, mirrors, clocks, many intriguing candleholders, wall decorations and metal furniture. Nothing is too large — Richard's numerous projects have included complete fitting of shop and café interiors, several of which have become well known landmarks in the London area.

EXHIBITION OF CERAMICS

1

2

3

1. John Chipperfield (Schomberg)
2. Jill Holland (Mid Cornwall)
3. Mike Goddard (Schomberg)
4. Andrew Mason (Blakesley)
5. Suzie Marsh (Mid Cornwall)

4

5

ARTWISE

24 Cotham Hill, Cotham, Bristol 6, Avon (0272) 467843 Fax (0272) 507573

Open Tuesday to Saturday 9.30am - 5.30pm

Artwise caters for the growing public demand for unusual works of quality and originality at prices to suit all pockets.

It started in early 1992 as an extension of the services offered by Studio International Limited, (a Gallery which specialises in contemporary Fine Art).

It is already a veritable cornucopia of fine etchings, prints, posters and three dimensional work including: studio ceramics, glass, sculpture, papier mache, candlesticks, mirrors and dried flowers, and is carefully managed by Gloria Armstrong, who has created a friendly and accessible environment for the lover of beautiful things.

The initial concept was, and still is, to develop an outlet for the work of artists, craftspeople and printmakers who make beautiful and

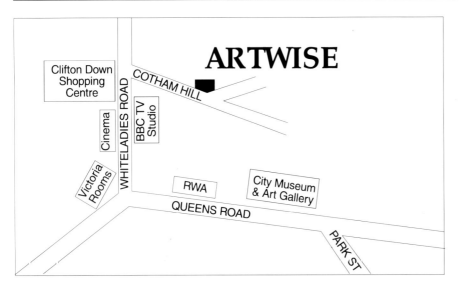

unusual objet d'arts in very limited quantities or as unique items.

Artwise also offers a custom framing service at very competitive prices, drawing on the skills and experience of the Gallery's in- house framing facilities.

The range of stock is continually expanding and changing so if any artist or craftsperson feels we might like their work please don't hesitate to get in contact.

The shop is situated on Cotham Hill, one of the more interesting parts of North West Bristol which runs off the busy Whiteladies Road.

RICHARD BALLINGER

Richard is a self-taught artist who, through commitment and hard work, has become one of the finest exponents of papier mache in Britain. His vessels, formed on hand made moulds or found objects, are mainly influenced by Mycenaean or early South American pottery.

The strength of these early culture forms are the perfect context for Richard to demonstrate his extraordinary skill. He is primarily influenced by such artists as Paul Klee, William Scott and the Mexican painter Rufino Tamayo. His work is consequently colourful and exciting, and yet it has an inherent subtlety distinguishing it from that of his contemporaries.

Richard's work has been well exhibited throughout the British Isles, and can now be seen at Artwise, where trade enquiries are welcome.

WENDY LOVEGROVE

Wendy Lovegrove cannot remember exactly when she first began to draw and paint, but knows it gradually became an essential ingredient in her busy life.

Born in Somerset, she completed her full time education in Bristol, after which she travelled widely.

Wendy now lives and works in Bristol. Her interest in the West Country landscape and the animal life to be found therein is reflected in her watercolours and etchings.

Although she has no formal training in Fine Art, Wendy has developed her own individual style full of movement and humour which has captivated the hearts of many who see her work.

You may see examples of her work at Artwise in Bristol, who also welcome trade enquiries.

MARTHA ALLEN

In 1980 Martha Allen graduated from the Bath Academy of Fine Art in ceramics. Since then she has lived and worked in Bath producing an unusual range of ceramic ware and sculpture.

Martha's strength lies in her modelling and sculptural ability, combined with an extraordinary imagination. She has produced several unusual puppet shows and has exhibited her sculpture in Art Galleries and at Art Fairs around the country.

Illustrated here is a pair of candlesticks which is typical of her modestly priced range of work which includes wall mounted plant holders, platters and masks.

Her work can be viewed at Artwise, where trade enquiries are welcome.

LOUISE GILBERT SCOTT

Trained at St Albans and London, Louise worked as an art therapist and ceramics teacher in London before moving to the west country where she has now established her studio.

Her colourful and highly individual small plates, decorated in vibrant abstract colour glazes, are represented in public and private collections including the Contemporary Art Society. Her work has been featured on TV, in Peter Lane's book *Ceramic Form*, and has been the subject of editorial in Crafts Magazine; Ceramics Monthly; Arts Review; Options Magazine; and Country Homes and Interiors. Her exhibitions include Chelsea Crafts Fair; the Vortex Gallery; Anatol Orient; and the Cre Gallery.

KEVIN de CHOISEY

Born in Cosford 1954. Between 1974 and 1979 he took a diploma in Vocational Pottery at Harrow School of Art, studying under Michael Casson OBE, Walter Keeler and Colin Pearson.

Between 1978 and 1980 Kevin spent time in New Mexico and Arizona studying pueblo Indian pottery. Subsequently he returned to America in 1984 to work as a potter and designer for the Rowe Pottery Works, Winconsin.

In 1988 Kevin established his own workshop, Moriah Pottery, where he drew upon his experience of the pueblos in making burnished pit fire ware, developing a range of stained and burnished earthen ware. Family affairs brought him back to England in 1990. He now lives and works in Bristol.

His continuing life long interest in low fired ware is represented here in Raku. Kevin de Choisey's work can be seen at Artwise. Trade enquiries are welcome.

THE BLAKESLEY GALLERY

Barton House, Blakesley, Nr Towcester, Northamptonshire (0327) 860282

Open Wednesday to Sunday inclusive 10am - 5pm. At other times by appointment.

The Blakesley Gallery was established in the village of Blakesley thirteen years ago and moved from its original site to Barton House in 1991 when the present owners took over.

The Gallery is situated in beautiful old barns behind a lovely 17th century Northamptonshire stone farmhouse which is next door to the Bartholomew Arms public house in the High Street.

George and Romayne Wisner have lived in Blakesley since the Gallery began and have closely followed its progress. Last year they heard that the Gallery was for sale as the owner wanted to retire. Without a moment's hesitation they offered to take it over, convert the old barns behind their house, and transfer the Gallery 200

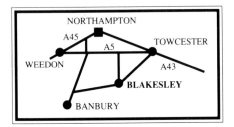

yards down the High Street. This was achieved with the Gallery being closed for only one week.

Both worked for the BBC as set and costume designers, so were well used to searching out craftsmen and one-off makers. The Gallery has now become a full-time occupation and more artists and craftspeople are able to exhibit in the two-monthly mixed exhibitions.

Each exhibition features work from at least fifteen painters, four or five ceramicists, two or three jewellers, plus sculpture, glass, metalwork, furniture and wood. Regular artists include Peter Newcombe, Paul Evans, D Rothwell Bailey, Dennis Page and Wendy Jelbert. There is also work by Nick and Rita Hodges, Andrew Mason, Mariette Voke, Joanna Howells and Martyn Pugh. The aim is for choice both in price and style, but always with an eye to quality.

In the heart of rural Northamptonshire, Blakesley is one of the prettiest villages. Its nearest town is Towcester, famous for its horse racing and its Heskeths and only four miles from Silverstone, home of the Motor Racing Grand Prix. Easily accessible from the M1 and new M40, Blakesley and the Gallery is the ideal place for a visit.

NICHOLAS AND RITA HODGES

Nicholas and Rita Hodges studied sculpture at Newcastle University and after a period in London moved to Oxfordshire to start a business in furniture design and making.

They have since been continuously commissioned for their unique style of both indoor and outdoor work in a variety of materials. They have also exhibited widely in this country and abroad.

Their work falls broadly into two categories. Nicholas has developed a market for his garden furniture of mainly one-off pieces for many private gardens; he has exhibited regularly with the Oxford Gallery and at Blakesley.

Their interior work is designed and made in partnership, which brings together a whole range of ideas and skills. The range is expansive and can be seen in dining room furniture, chests of drawers etc. and their speciality of decorative mirror frames. These bring together the skills of draughtsmanship, marquetry and craftsmanship.

MARIETTE VOKE
Garden Ceramics

Born in 1963, I studied ceramics in Cornwall and set up my first workshop in the mid eighties in Bristol. I am now living and working in the Forest of Dean.

I work in stoneware clay, making a range of work for gardens, including large pots, birdbaths, sundials and wall plaques.

All my work is individually hand built using methods of coiling and slab construction; shapes are kept simple and strong. The pieces are often decorated with incised lettering using quotations which relate to gardens, seasons, the weather, and for birbaths and sundials, water and time.

An interest in natural history inspires the making of fossils and shells, and lizards, frogs, birds and insects which are individually modelled on to each piece.

The work is fired to 1300 C which makes the clay resistant to frost; the flames of the kiln toast the clay, giving it a warm golden-brown colour; lettering and details are often painted with coloured clays in subtle shades of green, blue, coral and yellow.

ANDREW MASON
Unique handmade ceramics

During five years as a professional craft potter, Andrew Mason has developed a unique style of ceramics. The pieces are handmade and finished in their entirety at his studio in Stone, Staffordshire.

Using traditional methods, the majority of the work is thrown on the potters wheel. Whilst the throwing process takes place, balance and proportion are carefully, sometimes intuitively, determined.

Once through the initial making stage, the distinctive form of the pottery stands as evidently classical, possessing a particular elegance and poise.

Finally, using either Earthenware or Raku firing methods, a rich, lustrous and colourful glazed surface is produced, lending the work a contemporary appeal. The complementary alliance of form and colour bestows the pots with an exceptional presence and vitality.

'My work as a potter is enjoyable and constantly stimulating, and I believe will continue to surprise me with new discoveries. The pursuit of excellence is a compelling challenge.'

In recent years he has gained considerable recognition through exhibiting at selected Craft Council events in Britain and the United States.

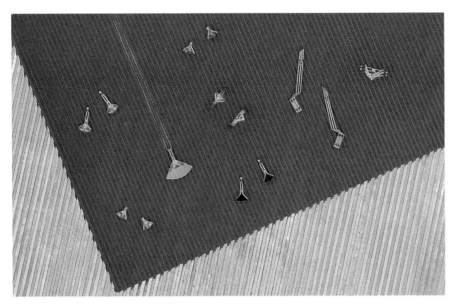

MARTYN PUGH

The style of Martyn Pugh's work is simple elegance and clean lines. His pieces require a high level of skill and attention to detail.

In his Jewellery Collection he uses silver, gold and platinum, with unusually shaped precious and semi-precious stones to create a wide choice. Simple or complex, delicate or bold, their designs reflect the precision of the techniques employed in their creation.

The Silver Collection is based upon a similar philosophy, combining function with elegance. This is evident in such pieces as the silver and crystal tableware, and the range of gifts for special occasions.

When working to commission, his expertise, integrity and interest in his clients ensures the same personal attention whether you plan to spend £25 or £25,000. He always allows time for careful discussions with each client before producing an idea. Only when mutual agreement has been reached over the design does he proceed with the piece.

JOANNA HOWELLS

Born in 1960, Joanna's first career was in medicine — she took a BA in Medical Sciences at Cambridge University. However, in 1984 she decided to pursue full time her love of ceramics. She went to the renowned studio pottery course at Harrow College of Higher Education, from where she graduated with distinction. She then set up her studio in London and has been exhibited widely since then. In 1991 she became a member of the prestigious Craft Potters Association.

After a period of experimentation, Joanna decided to work in porcelain, being attracted to the intrinsic beauty of the clay itself, particularly its purity and translucency. She decorates using slips in a wide variety of tones of blue, from very pale to deep midnight blues. In addition, some of the pieces are taken after glazing and painted with lustres and 18ct gold. They are then given a third firing, creating very special and rich effects.

Much of her inspiration comes from the natural world and she combines this with her appreciation of the great pottery traditions. Sea themes, the planets, and the beauty of flowers all feature in her designs. Also humour is rarely far away, as can be seen in the smiling faces of the fish, crab, seahorse and sun motifs.

Joanna welcomes the challenge to create new designs to commission. She also offers a personalisation service for wedding gifts and gifts for special occasions.

THE CRAFTSMAN GALLERY

8 High Street, Ditchling, East Sussex BN6 8TA (0273) 845246

The ancient village of Ditchling, 9 miles north of Brighton, is one of a string of villages tucked under the South Downs. It is a charming place to visit, with mellow houses dating from Tudor times, and is a particularly appropriate place for a craft gallery because of its association with the art and craft movement early this century. People still have stories to tell of Eric Gill and Hilary Peplar, of calligrapher Edward Johnston, painter Frank Brngwyn, and the school of weaving where Ethel Mairet welcomed students from all over the world.

At The Craftsman Gallery, I have tried since opening in 1975 to maintain a standard of craftsmanship that would not discredit the traditions of Ditchling. There is a constantly changing display of some of the finest work of Sussex artists and craftsmen. Etchings, prints and watercolours interpreting the Sussex landscape are complemented by ceramics and turned wood, jewellery and some textiles. Many, though by no means all of the makers, are members of the Guild of Sussex Craftsmen.

A potter myself, with my wheel in the gallery and my workshop behind it, I know the importance of displaying work well. I try to ensure a good standard of display for a range of work which may be decorative, or may be intended primarily for practical use, or may be both, but which is always well made and reasonably priced.

I have some information on local craftsmen and on exhibitions, so that if visitors' needs cannot be met by work in the gallery, then I may be able to direct them to individual craftsmen who may be ready to undertake special commissions.

Jill Pryke

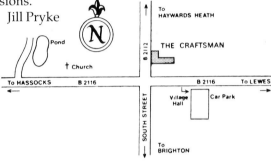

JILL PRYKE
Potter

Jill Pryke studied at Wimbledon School of Art (NDD in Pottery) and went on to gain her Art Teacher's Certificate at London University Institute of Education. However, most of what is relevant to her work now was learned during her years teaching both children and adults, first at Sutton, Surrey, and then in Hove and Hassocks, Sussex.

She set up her workshop at The Craftsman Gallery in Ditchling in 1975, throwing pots in red earthenware. She has developed a range of pots for daily use and for decoration, including a variety of candleholders — light seen through pierced work and cut-away openings always seems doubly attractive. Her work is characterised by soft green and blue glazes. She often decorates her pots with designs based on natural patterns and textures, using the sgraffito technique of scratching through one layer of glaze to reveal the colour underneath. She also accepts commissions for commemorative plates and bowls with inscriptions. Jill has been a member of the Guild of Sussex Craftsmen almost from its beginning and has exhibited with the Guild all over Sussex.

ROMOLA JANE
Ceramic Sculpture

Romola individually models people, birds and animals. They may be single figures or family groups, one bird or a pair in a bush, a single hound or a composite group. They vary in size from two to fifteen inches high.

Generally they have a bocage of flowering bushes which serves to frame the figures and also helps them to stand up. Most are opaque white glazed and painted in vibrant greens and blues with touches of yellow and pink. They make delightful dresser pieces in the Staffordshire tradition.

Romola also enjoys religious subjects such as Madonnas, nativity groups and patron saints; she has recently undertaken several larger mural compositions made in sections for church, school or hospital.

ROBERT R GREENHALF RBA SWLA

Robert was born in 1950 at Haywards Heath, Sussex. He studied at Eastbourne and Maidstone Colleges of Art, graduating in 1971 with a Diploma in Art and Design. He now lives with his wife Sally and son Jack near Rye, Sussex.

His drypoints, etchings and watercolours usually depict landscape, wildlife, or domestic animals. The etchings usually employ only one plate but are typically printed in eight to twelve colours. His drypoints are printed in a single colour and handcoloured later with watercolour. Great emphasis is placed upon observing and sketching in the field and his watercolours are usually painted directly from life.

He was elected a member of the Society of Wildlife Artists in 1981 and of the Royal Society of British Artists in 1982.

'Twentieth Century Wildlife Artists' by Nicholas Hammond, published in 1986, contains a chapter on Robert's work, and 'Drawing Birds' by John Busby contains a number of examples of his sketches and watercolours.

His work has been exhibited in many galleries and exhibitions throughout the UK and in Switzerland, France, Holland, and the USA.

JUDITH FISHER NDD ATC
Ceramics

Judith Fisher is a member of the Craft Potters' Association and the Guild of Sussex Craftsmen. She studied fine art and illustration at Brighton College of Art, followed by a year at Goldsmith College, London, where she became interested in three-dimensional work. Having been making ceramics professionally for several years, she began specialising in Raku since moving into the Sussex countryside five years ago.

Individual wheel-thrown vases are withdrawn from the red-hot kiln with long tongs whilst the glaze is still molten, and smothered in sawdust or other organic matter. The process is very dramatic, with plenty of flame, acrid smoke and a high breakage level. Glazes containing copper oxide undergo partial 'reduction', producing exciting colour variations, from turquoise to pink and bronze. Other pieces receive a special peel-away coating beforehand, resulting in an unglazed surface, veined and spotted by the smoking process.

The ware which successfully survives the intense thermal shock is porous with a surface often crazed and scarred by tong marks, but each piece is unique and can sometimes be beautiful.

CLARE McFARLANE
Living Ceramics

Born in 1964 in Nigeria, Clare's interest in plants and animals stems from her early childhood in Nigeria where the wildlife is plentiful and varied. Clare and her sister were taken on many excursions to look for plants by their father who is a botanist.

They returned to England when Clare was seven. At secondary school she started to do pottery in the small pottery room at the school. She had previously liked drawing, but soon began to prefer the 3-dimensional media.

In 1982 she started a two year Higher BATEC diploma in Ceramics at Croydon College, after completing a one year foundation course at Hastings College. In 1984 she left college and rented a workshop near Uckfield. To start with, she had a part-time job, but in 1987 she began working full-time for herself. She concentrates on the more popular animals such as cats, frogs, chickens, pigs and sheep. Clare sells to many retail outlets and exhibits in some galleries.

Her work is slip-cast in semi-porcelain, bisque fired, then hand painted and fired again to stoneware and porcelain temperatures. Many glazes have been discovered by accident, and many are difficult to reproduce exactly the same as previous pieces.

Many designs are modelled from life i.e. most cat designs are from her own pets. Photographs and drawings are also used as reference material.

The original model is done in clay. Then a plaster mould is made around the model (often in several pieces, so that the casts from the mould can be taken out in one piece). When the mould is finished, it is taken apart and allowed to dry before being put back together and used.

Clare usually glazes her work, but she also has a more natural finish, which is done by first firing on lustres, then by smoking pieces in sawdust. This finish emphasises the detail in her work, instead of covering it up, which glazes tend to do. Clare is currently working on ways to introduce more colours into the smoked pieces, and has recently been accepted as a provisional member of the Guild of Sussex Craftsmen.

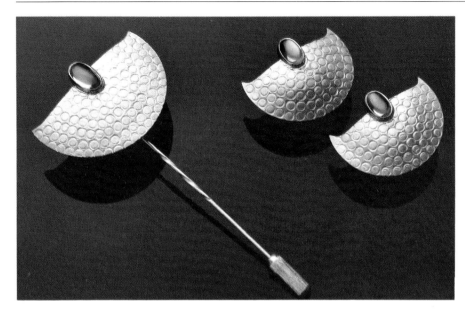

GUEN PALMER
Jewellery Designer

After graduating from Central School of Art and Design in 1978, I worked for several years in the jewellery manufacturing trade both in Africa and in the UK.

Now settled in the village of Ditchling, Sussex, I aim to produce exclusive jewellery that is individual, wearable and affordable.

I use mainly 18ct gold and silver, but also exotic materials, gemstones and pearls where appropriate.

Each piece is made by hand using traditional methods, together with specialised techniques that develop as part of the design process.

Most of the work consists of 'one-off' pieces but also some limited editions.

Commission enquiries are welcomed.

EXHIBITION OF WOOD

2

3

1

1. Michael O'Donnell (Working Tree)
2. Hayley Smith ((Schomberg)
3. Bert Marsh (Gowan)
4. Mike Scott (New Ashgate)

4

Photo: Hayley Smith

COURTYARD GALLERY

The Gallery for Contemporary Jewellery

Bath Terrace, Leckhampton, Cheltenham, Glos. (0242) 221711

Open Monday to Saturday 9.30am - 5.30pm (Closed Sundays and Bank Holidays)

I n 1987, upon reaching that certain age when 'life begins', Courtyard Gallery was opened in Bath Terrace, Leckhampton, Cheltenham by the proprietor Jim Jones, a former Ceramics and Art teacher. The Gallery stands alongside his wife Veronica's Photographic Portrait Studio.

The premises in Cheltenham are as nearly perfect for the two specialist businesses as it is possible to get, being surrounded by a large well-used car park.

Throughout the summer of 1987 Jim helped with the improvements and layout of the attractive Courtyard area, to give the Gallery a pleasant ambience. Whilst digging out the floor of the Gallery area, the original flagstones were discovered and almost every one was initialled and numbered by the stonemasons.

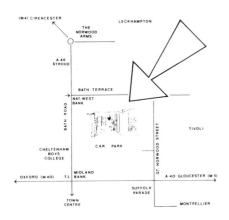

These have been sensitively incorporated as part of the overall design of the Courtyard area.

The Gallery has a high reputation, displaying a wide range of contemporary designer-made jewellery. Along with the jewellery, the regularly changing monthly exhibitions include a 'guest' artist or printmaker, studio glass or ceramics.

These all combine to produce exciting lively exhibitions, often with a theme, and all work is for sale at a wide range of prices.

Past exhibiting artists have included Rowland Hilder OBE, Elizabeth Blackadder OBE, RA, David Tindle RA and the late Valerie Thornton RE.

It is the aim of the Gallery to help present jewellery, prints and contemporary crafts, all of the highest quality, in an attractive imaginative way to the public.

KERYN EVELY
Enameller

The medium of vitreous enamel on metal, usually silver in my case, has held my interest since I first encountered it nearly twenty years ago. At that time I had just finished teacher training, although I had also been attending evening classes in jewellery making. A few years on, I decided to pursue this interest further in case I later regretted not doing so! I studied at Glasgow School of Art, graduating in 1982.

In my post-graduate year I concentrated on enamelling. In the meticulous technique required for enamelling and also the smallness of scale within which the colours and design have to be organised, I found a medium of expression which really suited me. Since leaving Glasgow I have worked with Rodger Drew, who specialises in chased silverware, from our home in Perthshire. Occasionally we collaborate, combining chased work with enamel.

I make mainly jewellery, especially brooches, ear-rings, neckpieces and cuff-links, but also some small scale silverware such as boxes, bowls and beakers. I have a slowly evolving range of designs, some of which I call my 'perennials', and these are the nearest I come to a production line.

The themes in my work are derived from two main sources, natural forms and decorative art from ancient (Egyptian wall paintings, Minoan frescoes) and not so ancient times. Illustrated here is a Japanese lady brooch set. As much of my work is produced for exhibitions, this encourages as well as permits the changes in theme and style. I use cloisonné wires, foils and engraving to create texture under the transparent enamel, and I enjoy using bright contrasting colours or gradually shaded, muted tones as appropriate.

I am a member of the British Society of Enamellers, the Society of Designer Craftsmen, and 'Flux', the Glasgow Fine Metals Group.

ANNETTE JOHNSON SWA NS
Painter, Etcher

Annette Johnson was born in London and has lived by the river front in Greenwich for the last 20 years.

She started painting whilst living in Boston, America, and has since studied at Sir John Cass College of Art and Etching at Morley College. She has her own studio where she works as a full-time painter/etcher.

She is a member of the Society of Women Artists, the National Society of Painters Sculptors and Printmakers, and the Greenwich Printmakers Association. Her work is in galleries throughout the country. She is a regular exhibitor at the Mall Galleries, Westminster Central Halls, and also the Royal Academy.

Her work for the past few years has been botanical etchings. She works on copperplate with hard and soft ground for the line and aquatint for the tonal quality. She also does all her own printing. Her spare time is spent growing and painting flowers.

JEANNE WERGE-HARTLEY

The work of Jeanne Werge-Hartley encompasses both jewellery and small scale silver- and goldsmithing. It is designed and made in 18 carat gold, silver, precious and semi-precious stones, anodised niobium and tantalum, and cloisonné enamel. Pieces often include two or more of these elements to produce decorative and polychromatic effects.

Recent collections of enamelled pieces include brooches, ear-rings, rings and necklaces, which have been inspired by the decorative quality of the paintings of Gustav Klimpt. The jewellery is made in silver, 18 carat gold, and includes both cloisonné and bastaille enamelling. 18 carat necklaces, rings and ear-rings also feature in Jeanne's work, often with interesting semi-precious stones such as grey blue iolites, soft dusky pink tourmalines, and the more unusual peacock blue topaz.

Although Jeanne sells work through the Courtyard Gallery, Cheltenham, and other galleries specialising in jewellery, she also has frequent exhibitions, and welcomes commissions which evolve through a close client/designer-maker relationship.

Jeanne is a Freeman of the Worshipful Company of Goldsmiths and a Founder Member of the Designer Jewellers' Group.

GLYNN THOMAS RE

Born 1946 Cambridge. Studied illustration and printmaking at the Cambridge Art School. Taught printmaking at the Ipswich School of Art 1967-79; is now a full-time artist living in Suffolk and is a member of the Royal Society of Painter Printmakers.

Glynn now works almost exclusively in the medium of etching. This process enables him to express his multiplicity of ideas which entail observing topographical and landscape details in various ways, which might include tilting the picture plane and viewing images from various aspects which co-ordinate into a 'realistic image', although conventional perspective is not totally abandoned. By employing these ideas he feels he achieves a greater empathy with the chosen subject.

Normally, coloured etchings are printed by using a number of plates, but Glynn's coloured etchings are from just one original plate. Small pieces of muslin are used to ink up the plate in various colours and these merge to give subtle colour variations. Great patience and skill are therefore required to achieve the desired effect, and for editioning. Each inking of the plate allows the artist to print only one copy at a time.

ELEANOR BARTLEMAN

While studying ceramics at Glasgow School of Art in the seventies, I came across the story of Reynard the Fox — originally one of Aesop's fables but very popular in the Middle Ages. I became fascinated by the sinister undercurrents of these seemingly simple rustic tales, and by the many pictures and carvings left by the medieval craftsmen.

For a time, much of my work revolved around the dastardly deeds of Reynard the Fox and then encompassed other ancient stories. I took ideas from manuscripts and played around with them to make them my own.

Applying these ideas to the ceramic medium, I wanted to find a method which would reflect the feel and colours of medieval drawings. I wanted the finished pieces to be small, mysterious and jewel-like. I stained the earthenware in a variety of colours and used the transparent glaze to pick out details rather than glaze the whole piece. The use of lustres and metals gave the final sparkle.

Over the years I have used many different sources as the basis of the creative process. The Commedia dell'Arte, the writings of Gerald of Wales, and the Bible are just a few of the starting points. This may involve making a complete exhibition based on a whole story, or more likely I will find one tiny detail which I can develop into part of my own mythology. The range of work stretches from small trinket boxes through to larger ornamental pieces.

I left art school in 1979 and set up on my own. I have moved my workshop frequently but I hope that I am now permanently based in North Devon.

ELLIS PALMER
Designer Jeweller

There has been a long period of development and interest in the designing and making of her jewellery, together with a similar period of time teaching this subject as a part-time lecturer.

Many of her designs and ideas have a strong association with baroque and theatrical themes. The use of a range of established materials, such as gold and oxidised silver, accompanied by precious and semi-precious stones, has in recent years been linked with bone and suitably shaped fossils.

These have at times formed designs with primeval characteristics.

Her work is enhanced by a delicate use of natural forms to complement her creative use of metal.

Some of her works are consciously produced as miniature sculptures and are displayed as such when not worn.

She has exhibited widely in London, abroad and many provincial galleries.

Her resignation from all teaching commitments has finally allowed total involvement, working from her workshop at Horndean, Hants, her reputation as a jeweller of distinctive qualities is now growing.

CAROLINE WHYMAN

Caroline Whyman went to art school with the intention of becoming a painter, but as soon as she started to work with clay she knew that she wanted to be a potter. She went to Camberwell Art School where there was a strong bias towards studio pottery, and she was one of the last group of students to be taught by Lucie Rie and Hans Coper.

Her first workshop was at Camden Lock where she worked for nine years with stoneware and porcelain — throwing domestic ware, coiling large planters, and slabbing vases and boxes. Being an urban potter, it was easier to develop her work using an electric kiln, and she became involved in developing colourful glazes as an alternative to the more usual browns and creams. This research led her to experiment with porcelain because the whiteness of the clay enhanced and brightened the colours and she found that she enjoyed the precision with which porcelain could be thrown and turned.

Her next workshop, in Islington, away from the immediate contact with the public, saw the development of more one-off pieces; taking ideas and working them through as a series. After a visit to Japan in 1980, and inspired by the richness of the textile designs, Caroline began to incorporate decoration into her stoneware bowls using coloured slips and paper resist.

Now in her third workshop in south London, she works exclusively in porcelain, making teapots, cups and bowls, as well as unusual vases, large dishes and bowls, and carefully made lidded boxes. These are glazed with a wide variety of her own glazes, from a starkly simple stained crackle glaze which emphasises the simplicity of the form, through a range of blues and pinks, to the complex underglaze blue decoration which is further decorated with precious metal lustres. The designs and rich colours of the lustres were a direct result of a recent trip to India where the vibrancy and strength of the colours and textures made a lasting impression.

SIMON DREW GALLERY

Simon and Caroline Drew, 13 Foss Street, Dartmouth, Devon TQ6 9DR (0803) 832832

Open Monday to Saturday 9am - 5pm

We established our gallery in 1981 when we took over what had once been a Cranks Health Food shop in Dartmouth town centre.

Over the years, the gallery has grown from one room to three rooms, enabling us to show a wider range of pictures and ceramics. At first we also stocked glassware and turned wood, but our increasing interest in and enjoyment of ceramics led us to specialise in pottery in the crafts section of the gallery.

As well as original pictures, prints, cards and books by Simon Drew, we permanently show the work of potters working in the UK. There is always a wide variety of earthenware, stoneware, porcelain and raku, some in the form of

functional pottery and some purely sculptural or decorative.

We hold two or three major exhibitions each year; these are sometimes solo exhibitions or work by an individual potter and sometimes group shows, usually on a theme.

The ceramics shown in the gallery include work by the following exhibitors: Michael and Barbara Hawkins, Liz Riley, Claire Edkins, Laurel Keeley, Hilary Laforce, Donald and Jacqueline Mills, Anna Lambert, Colin Kellam, Andrew Mason, Nicky Smart and Lorraine Taylor, Lorna Jackson-Currie, Philippa de Burlet, Peter Beard, Nick Chapman, Rob Whelpton, Vicki Longbottom, Sara Pearch, Jenny Beavan, Sabina Teuteberg, Willie Carter, Yasaharu Tajima-Simpson, Penny Tajima-Simpson, Morgen Hall, Svend Bayer, John Pollex, David White, Liz Beckenham, Chris Speyer, Nichola Werner, Jane Mobach, Jill Holland, Millie Wood-Swanepoel, Lawson E Rudge, Lawson C Rudge, Dillon Rudge, Keza Rudge, Sue Schwarz, Amanda King, Belinda Brayshaw, David and Rosemary Ashby, Antonia Salmon.

SIMON DREW

Simon Drew's pictures are on permanent show in the gallery. Often based on a still life subject, they are pen and ink drawings using coloured inks and crayon.

He has written and illustrated several books of nonsense verse and also produces prints and greetings cards.

The book titles include: A Book of Bestial Nonsense, Nonsense in Flight, Still Warthogs Run Deep, The Puffin's Advice, Cat with Piano Tuna.

NICK CHAPMAN

Nick Chapman was born in 1954 in South Wales. He first started making pots in his early teens in the pottery room of the London remand home where his mother worked. With classmates ranging from pickpockets to murderers, he struggled with clay until at last he was making pots.

After school he spent some time working at Ray Finch's workshop, then worked in several potteries in England, the Channel Islands and France before going to Harrow School of Art to attend the studio pottery course.

On leaving Harrow, Nick went to work for Clive Bowen at the Shebbear Pottery, where he met Charmian Harris, the jeweller, now his wife.

In 1978 they moved to North Devon where they still live. Nick's work is highly decorated using his own tortuous methods; his main trouble is that he needs more time to finish his intricate vases, candlesticks and plates. Nick's work has been exhibited at the Simon Drew Gallery for a few years, where he has also had two solo exhibitions.

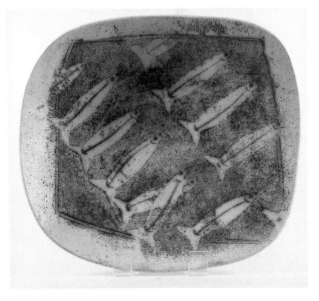

LAUREL KEELEY

Laurel Keeley obtained an Honours degree in English at Exeter University and an MA at Toronto University in the 1970s before turning to pottery when she studied Ceramics at Exeter College of Art and Design.

Laurel runs her own workshop in Exeter, where she produces decorative stoneware.

She has won several British Crafts Council awards and her work is on permanent show in the Simon Drew Gallery, where she has also held solo exhibitions.

DANSEL GALLERY

Rodden Row, Abbotsbury, Dorset (0305) 871515

Dansel was started by Danielle and Selwyn Holmes from their home near Bridport in 1976. They were both trained at Kingston Art School specialising in 3D Design, particularly furniture. They began by making one-off pieces to commission. Soon they expanded and moved in 1979 to their present workshop in Abbotsbury where they developed a range of smaller items.

Dansel Gallery now displays and sells other British craftsmen's work as well as their own, all of which is made in a large variety of hardwoods. The work is of a high standard and of contemporary design.

One-off bowls, boxes and cabinets are featured, as well as a range of kitchen, desk and domestic ware. Commissions can be taken for pieces of furniture designed by Dansel as well as by other craftsmen. They have a toy section including only handmade wooden toys, and an area devoted to books about trees, woodworking and design.

The Gallery is housed in a carefully restored thatched stable block which is around 300 years old and uses old wooden stable doors to close over internal picture windows.

Dansel is open 7 days a week from 10 to 5 all year round. There is a large car park and it is easy to find near the centre of the village on the main Bridport to Weymouth road (B3157).

Dansel Gallery is well worth a visit due to the unusual nature and quality of the woodwork displayed, as well as its interesting location in a very picturesque village. It is a good example of modern ideas blending comfortably in ancient surroundings.

QUARTET DESIGNS

Dansel have developed a range of children's puzzles and three-dimensional toys alongside their more serious woodwork, which is marketed under the name of Quartet Designs.

Three-dimensional effects are created on essentially flat pieces of plywood by the delicate use of colour, giving each piece more depth. The emphasis is on the educational aspect of colour, size and space comprehension. The complete range of designs can be used as teaching aids in pre-school education. Easily recognisable animal shapes are chosen, handmade on best quality birch plywood, finished with non-toxic paints and varnishes.

Dansel find the use of colour very stimulating alongside working with wood in its natural state where grain patterns often determine an item's design and use.

KEVIN TRY
Furniture

Kevin Try was born in Berkshire and now lives in Devon where he established his workshop five years ago.

Having studied fine craftsmanship at Rycotewood College in Oxfordshire, Kevin now produces mainly one-off pieces of furniture to commission for the home. Other work includes some small batch productions as well as some commercial pieces.

All furniture is to original designs incorporating the needs and personal preferences of the client whenever necessary.

Construction is mainly in solid hardwoods and also decorative veneers. These are often contrasted with other materials such as metals, stone, glass, leather and fabrics.

Photo: Brian B Eveleigh

PERRY LANCASTER
John Fox Workshop

John Fox Woodcarving and Sculpture was founded in 1973 by the late John Fox and included a range of stylised carved wooden animals, with the emphasis being placed on cats, along with abstracts, torsos and figurines.

The beautiful highly-polished finish, together with a unique impressionistic style, soon earned John a reputation for quality and imagination which was the foundation of John Fox Woodsculpture.

Based in Cambridgeshire, Perry Lancaster, a pupil of John's for a number of years, continues to produce original John Fox Woodsculpture under the name of the John Fox Workshop and, using exactly the same methods of production, has added new items to the range.

Constantly striving to reach greater heights, Perry is always experimenting with wood and trying new ideas. These include stressed, charred, and painted woodsculpture which is very different from John Fox Woodsculpture, but the idea of constant refinement through production remains the same.

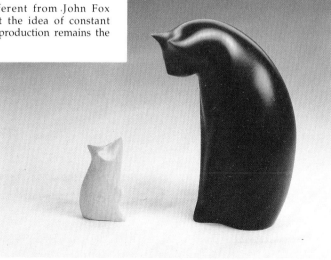

IAN WALLER
Wood Sculptor

Ian has worked with wood as a hobby since childhood, his other lifelong interest in nature often being the source of inspiration. In 1986 he decided to combine the two as his full time occupation, since when the variety and scope of subjects has gradually expanded. Wherever possible, his work is also based on his own photography.

He is perhaps best known at present for his exceptionally lifelike representations of waterfowl and other birds, including game birds and raptors. For this, almost grainless timbers are selected to facilitate the creation of the detailed feather pattern. The final stage is a painstaking gradual build-up of subtle blends of colour.

In constrast, a wide variety of timbers are used for various animal and human forms, where the grain of the wood and the finely polished surface are important features. This is an area of Ian's work which is currently expanding.

Since 1987 Ian's work has been exhibited at many galleries and shows and has generated a great deal of interest in the worlds of art, craft and television.

SIMON TEED
Furniture Designer and Maker

Simon started his career in furniture making at Rycotewood Furniture College and furthered his experience for three years with furniture maker Alan Peter OBE. This gave him a wide knowledge in the highest quality work both for individual commissions and prestigious organisations.

In 1989, with this experience behind him, Simon set up his own furniture-making business at Budleigh Salterton, Devon. Soon after this he was elected to the Devon Guild of Craftsmen, centred at Bovey Tracey, where he exhibits regularly.

Simon's work comprises mainly of individual commissions, but he also designs and makes pieces for exhibitions and local galleries.

Simon's uncomplicated views on design are reflected in his work, and the quality uncompromising. The adjacent photograph of a Hall Table with two concealed drawers shows the simple elegance of his work which allows the natural beauty of the wood to be appreciated.

Simon welcomes the opportunity to combine his own design ideas with those of a customer. He likes to use a wide range of woods in his work, but his concern for the rain forests prevents him from using timbers from environmentally threatened areas.

CHRISTOPHER VICKERS
Fine Wooden Boxes

Chris started making boxes whilst serving as an apprentice joiner. The love of precision and fine workmanship led him in 1983 to the London College of Furniture where he graduated with distinction. There followed several years working in London, as well as teaching cabinet making and exhibiting his own work. In 1987 Chris moved to Frome in Somerset in order to set up a workshop and home with his wife Jennifer.

For Chris, boxmaking is the ideal medium for displaying the natural beauty of the woods he uses, such as Walnut Burrs, Mulberry, Strawberry and Bog Oak. Sometimes combining silverwork, his boxes are often based on Victorian ideas but with 'arts and crafts' inspiration and fine craftsmanship.

Whilst happy to make to commission, Chris makes a wide range of boxes from 5 inch long perfume bottle cases to 18 inch long sewing boxes with inlaid lids, removable trays and hand-cut dovetails. Jewellery boxes of various types, writing cases, and a selection of mirrors complete the range that is aimed at providing something for everyone.

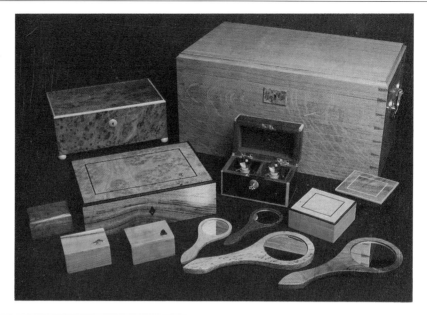

JOHN VARLEY
H & J Designs

Born in 1940, John made his first career in Agricultural Research and Project Management. In 1981 he moved to Dorset with his family and studied for two years at the renowned John Makepeace School for Craftsmen in Wood at Parnham.

He built his workshops and started his furniture business in 1983. Soon after this he was accepted as a full member of the Dorset Craft Guild. He has recently completed three years as Chairman of the Guild and has moved his workshops into the village of Abbotsbury.

John's work places emphasis on original, practical design in solid English hardwoods, worked and finished to high standards of craftsmanship. While he still likes to make some pieces of one-off furniture, more recently he has concentrated on taking up the challenge of bringing original design and high standards of craftsmanship to a wider range of people, both in the UK and overseas.

John's small family firm, H & J Designs, offers a creative selection of miniature clocks, desk accessories, and other gift items, all made and finished to a high standard and packed in attractive gift boxes.

Enthusiastic about design and problem solving, John relishes the opportunity of developing a new design to meet the particular challenge of a one-off presentation gift or a new repeat item. Suggestions are always welcome.

His lifelong love of wood and the possibilities it offers in design is obvious in his work, which he hopes, by being distributed through galleries and quality individual retail outlets, will bring the visual and tactile pleasures of solid wood to a wider public.

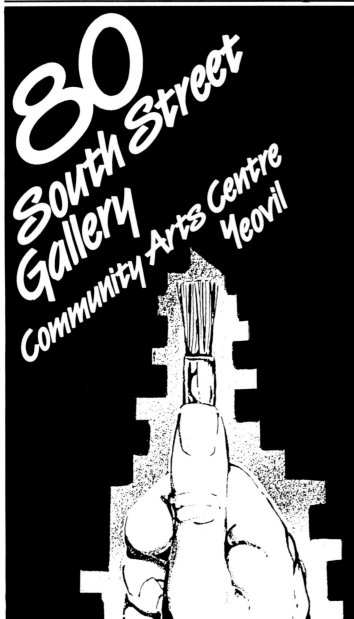

80 South Street Gallery
Community Arts Centre Yeovil

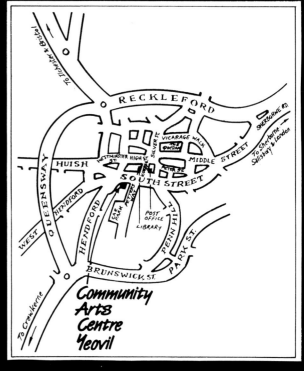

Community Arts Centre Yeovil

Opening Times
The gallery and coffee shop is open
Monday to Friday, 10.00-4.30,
Saturday 10.00-2.00. The Centre is
closed on Bank Holidays.

How to find us
80 South Street is centrally situated
near the library and adjacent to a
good sized car park.

FIRE & IRON GALLERY

Rowhurst Forge, Oxshott Road, Leatherhead, Surrey KT22 0EN (0372) 375148

Open Monday to Saturday 9am - 5pm throughout the year

Fire & Iron Gallery was set up in 1982 by the Quinnell family in response to a renaissance of British blacksmithing. The Quinnells, long established metalworkers, felt that there was a need for a good public space in which to show off not only the work being made in their own workshops, but also new and interesting metalwork designed and made by others. They set about converting the existing small showroom and outbuildings into 2,500 square feet of display space.

Fire & Iron has been selected for quality by the Crafts Council and exhibits and sells work by the world's best metalsmiths — sculpture, jewellery, candlesticks, bowls, furniture, fire baskets, fire backs, fire screens and mesh curtains, companion sets, chestnut roasters, log hoops, boot scrapers, door stops, hooks, paper weights, paper knives, book ends, clocks, lamps, lanterns, gates, door furniture, plant stands, flower pedestals, mirrors, wind chimes, wine racks, weathervanes, house signs and sundials from the United Kingdom, America, Australia, France, Italy, Spain, Norway, Finland, Germany, Switzerland, Poland, Czechoslovakia, Estonia and Russia.

At the preview of Sotheby's exhibition and auction '20th Century Ironwork' — over 200 pieces of contemporary metalwork were on show in our gallery and sculpture garden, one of the finest and most exciting collections ever assembled in this country.

We hold 4-6 special exhibitions each year. Demonstrations of metal-working techniques take place in a specially built arena, a new facility which enables members of the public to watch in safety and gain a greater understanding and appreciation of this exciting craft.

We also make to order, at any scale, from small domestic items to large architectural commissions. Fire & Iron Gallery works closely with and on the same site as Richard Quinnell Ltd., a highly successful company of metalworkers with extensive resources and fifty years of experience in this field. Richard Quinnell, MBE,MA,FRSA, works with his team of ten skilled blacksmiths and other men and women specialising in associated aspects of metalwork (gilding, shotblasting, painting, patination, casting, engraving, etc.) to create work of an extremely high standard, both in terms of workmanship and design. Why not come and see what we are doing? Whether you want to buy a fabulous wedding present, have a hinge repaired, commission a sculpture or gates for your castle, or just have a look around, we will be delighted to see you.

Lucy Quinnell

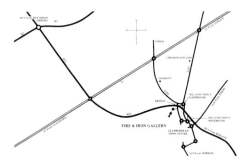

ADRIAN REYNOLDS

Adrian Reynolds designs and manufactures exclusive items to commission and also produces a commercial range of furniture and interior accessories for major retailers such as Liberty and Harvey Nichols.

Since completing his degree in Three Dimensional Design (BA Hons.) at West Surrey College of Art & Design, Adrian has established his own workshop in Shropshire and has exhibited his work at numerous shows, including the 'Creative Eye' exhibitions at Chelsea Town Hall, and 'Chelsea Comes to California' in the USA.

All of Adrian's work involves honest treatment of materials and is uniquely designed and finished with rigorous attention to detail. He uses techniques such as acid etching, hot forging and the colouration of titanium, and combines these skills with a variety of original ideas to create work that is both aesthetically and commercially successful.

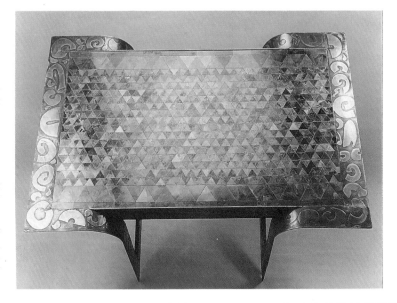

SUSAN MAY

Susan May was born in London in 1954. She studied jewellery at the Middlesex Polytechnic from 1972-1976, and from 1976-1977 worked for a manufacturing jeweller in Hatton Garden under the Goldsmiths' Apprenticeship Scheme. In 1977 she set up her own workshop with the aid of a Crafts Council grant. She also taught delinquent boys metalwork, woodwork and motor engineering in the East End.

In 1980 Susan worked in New York for three months, printing people's names on apples. From 1981-1985 she was a part time tutor at ILEA jewellery classes. Susan is on the Craft Council's Select Index. She is best known for her exquisite jewellery in cold-forged precious metals, but in recent years has been successfully experimenting with larger scale work in flame-cut, welded and hot-forged steel.

She has exhibited and sold work in Britain and America, including 'Creative Eye' at Chelsea and 'Chelsea Comes to California'.

Photo: Geoff Power

SARAH WILLIAMS MA (RCA)

Sarah is a recent graduate of the Royal College of Art, where she studied metalwork and jewellery. Whilst at the RCA she won a travel scholarship to Indonesia to study tribal art. During this trip Sarah became interested in Indonesian flora and fauna and was struck by how the tribespeople were so inextricably linked with their natural environment.

Her experiences inspired a collection of pieces which express certain fundamental aspects of nature: beauty, symmetry of form, tangibility, colour, decay and regeneracy.

The pieces are made using a relatively unusual technique called electroforming; a basic framework is constructed and then copper is deposited onto the surface. This method gives a strong, very substantial object made of copper, which is then patinated.

RACHEL RECKITT

At 84, Rachel Reckitt is the doyenne of British blacksmithing.

A sculptor and wood-engraver, she had always wanted to work with metal and attended blacksmithing courses in the 1960s. Thirty years on, her spectacular forged and welded sculptures continue to amaze her colleagues worldwide.

'I enjoy playing with fire, making a hard, difficult metal do what you want. Iron is the most satisfying and rewarding of metals; it has endless possibilities. The metal constantly develops your style and influences your artistic ideas'.

Rachel lives and works in Somerset.

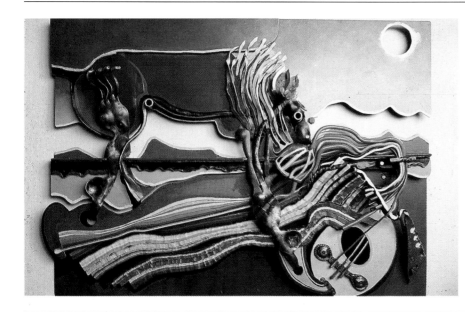

MICHAEL HENDERSON

Michael Henderson was born in Scotland in 1942, and studied at Bolton and Gloucester Colleges of Art in the 1960s. Since leaving college he has created a wide variety of contemporary paintings, and in 1987 formed 'Anvil Art' to develop his interest in combining blacksmithing and painting skills.

Michael lives and works in Dorset, using hot forging, argon/arc welding, gas cutting and power hammer techniques to produce sculptured wall panels and free standing pieces in steel, designed to be viewed in Public Art, architectural or gallery context. His work tends to be finished in spectacular high gloss colours, with only a few areas left in polished steel.

Michael has recently completed the construction and installation of two multi-coloured steel sculpture panels for the gateway of Highworth Community Golf Centre.

PAUL MARGETTS
Artist Blacksmith

Paul served a traditional four-year blacksmithing apprenticeship near his Worcestershire home before travelling extensively overseas. His time was spent working metals in several countries, including three years training rural smiths in Zimbabwe.

He returned to Britain and studied art and design at Birmingham Polytechnic before opening his own forge in Belbroughton.

Paul hot-forges steels and non-ferrous metals to his own innovative designs using both traditional and modern techniques. His work includes indoor functional sculpture such as fire baskets, candlestands, bookends, clocks and lighting as well as larger outdoor pieces such as sundials, weathervanes, gates, fountains, garden sculpture and furniture.

Recently Paul has been forging sculptures based on the human form; some pieces have African themes, inspired by his affection for that continent. He is also gaining a reputation for his semi-abstract bird sculptures.

His work has won many awards at shows during 1991 and 1992, and he has exhibited and sold work at The Barbican and Sotheby's.

FIRE AND IRON

EXHIBITION OF WOOD

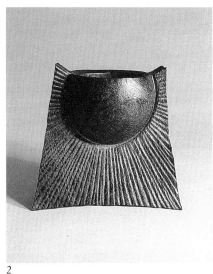

1. John Varley (Dansel)
2. Paul Clare (Working Tree)
3. John Mainwaring (Hitchcocks)
4. Richard Windley (Alpha)

THE GOWAN GALLERY

3 Bell Street, Sawbridgeworth, Hertfordshire CM21 9AR (0279) 600004

Open Tuesday to Saturday 10am - 5pm (Closed one week after Christmas)

The Gowan Gallery is a contemporary craft and art gallery in the small picturesque town of Sawbridgeworth on the Hertfordshire/Essex border. The 18th century shop has a long tradition as a jewellers and has been carefully renovated to provide a relaxed atmosphere whilst retaining the old display cabinets and original features.

The gallery is run by resident designer jeweller Joanne Gowan, who opened it in 1987, altering the shop layout to make the most of the 400 sq ft of space. Her aim is to offer quality craft and art works in a variety of media for collectors and a discerning public.

There is a continually changing display of work for sale including ceramics, glass, wood, jewellery, fine art, sculpture, and limited edition etchings. A selection of beautiful and unusual work is available by British designer makers and artists. One-off

and limited production pieces are exhibited by our foremost craftspeople and talented newcomers. Individual commissions to most of the artists can also be arranged.

The range of ceramics, glass and wood includes both functional and

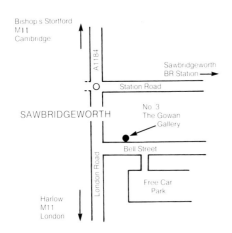

decorative pieces in a variety of styles with a wide price range. There is always a good selection of precious and non- precious designer jewellery in stock, as well as Joanne's own work, and commissioning an item of jewellery is made particularly easy as her workshop is situated within the gallery. Joanne is also pleased to arrange commissions to the other jewellers whose work is on display.

In addition to the display of framed works of art, there is a portfolio of unframed pieces enabling a larger selection of each artist's work to be shown. The gallery has a high quality bespoke framing service available, with over 100 frame mouldings to choose from, whether you already have something to frame or wish to buy something from the portfolio.

The gallery holds a number of exhibitions each year where half of the display area is used to show the work of a group of particular artists/ craftspeople. This allows the customer to choose from a wider collection of their work and usually lasts for three weeks. If you would like to receive details of these exhibitions and private view invitations, please write to be included on the mailing list.

The Gowan Gallery is selected for quality by the Crafts Council.

JOANNE GOWAN
Designer Jeweller

At her workshop within the Gowan Gallery, Joanne designs and makes fine precious jewellery, with most of her work being one-off designs and individual commissions. Elaborate 18 carat gold pieces are made by hand using different techniques including repoussé and forging. Curved, twisted, organic shapes are produced in her own particular style and often incorporate faceted or cabochon cut gemstones. Joanne also has a range of jewellery in silver with 18ct gold and works in platinum to order.

Individual pieces, wedding and engagement rings, are designed specially on consultation with the customer and made to commission. A selection of work in a wide price range is always on display at the gallery.

Joanne trained at Central School of Art and Design and received a BA (Hons) in Jewellery Design in 1985. She has been self-employed as a designer jeweller since 1986.

Joanne has exhibited her work at many galleries and fairs throughout this country, including the prestigious Goldsmiths' Fair. She has also exported work to Japan, and in 1990 was one of six British jewellers in an exhibition at Musee de Bellezza, Tokyo.

Photo: Graham Portlock

CAROLYN GENDERS
Ceramics

Carolyn Genders makes sculptural pots and plates. She deliberately chooses strong simple shapes for her work as she feels that the individual treatment of the surface of the pot is most successful on understated forms.

Having always enjoyed drawing and painting, Carolyn constantly refers to her sketchbooks for the inspiration needed to paint her pots. Using a wide range of vitreous coloured slips, she approaches her work much as a painter does his canvas; the result is colourful, lively and vibrant pieces that have many of the qualities of a painting with the added excitement of constant surprise provided by the element of the three-dimensional.

JULIET MAY
Decorative Mirrors

Juliet May produces a range of handmade and decorative mirrors which are constructed from papier maché on a wooden frame and then individually painted.

Juliet graduated from the Royal College of Art in 1988. Her work was mainly decorated glass, but having decided that the risk factor with a piece of glass was too great, she looked for another material to work in. Papier maché seemed ideal; it was flexible, it lent itself to decoration, it's 'green', and less breakable!

Combining papier maché with mirrors was a natural development which has proved to be successful. Her work has received much publicity and she makes mirrors for commission, exhibitions, and produces a range for sale in shops.

She takes her ideas from a variety of sources which include carnival and fairground art, Indian and Mexican design. Juliet's work is always ornamental and she aims to achieve a whimsical appearance.

RACHEL GOGERLY
Jewellery Designer and Enameller

As a professional jeweller based in York, Rachel specialises in enamelling, producing a collection of silver and vitreous enamel jewellery for men and women.

Using rich transparent enamel colours which are applied over hand-engraved patterns, her work is distinctive in design and quality. She also works in gold to commission, offering jewellery with a personal touch. Her exclusive range of jewellery includes necklaces, bracelets, brooches, ear-studs, ear-clips and drop ear-rings, rings, stick-pins, buttons, cuff-links, tie- tacks and tie-slides.

On completion of a four year BA Hons. degree course in Jewellery Design at Middlesex Polytechnic, Rachel took a short course in business studies before setting up her workshop in December 1986.

Since that time she has shown work in many exhibitions and fairs, including Chelsea Crafts Fair and Goldsmiths' Fair, as well as undertaking special commissions such as work for the Lord Mayor of York. In 1988 she won the regional finals of 'Livewire' and in 1989 was selected for 'First Impressions', an Arts Award scheme, where she appeared on Anglia TV.

BERT MARSH
Finely Turned Decorative Wooden Vessels

My life has been spent working with wood, and it is the love of it, coupled with a deep understanding of its ways, that has influenced all my work.

I select my materials from a wide variety of bland and exotic timbers, paying particular attention to natural defects, discoloration, and grain malformations. Sensitive turning exposes the textures, colour and patterns which are enhanced by meticulous finishing.

Many of my vessels are functional, but I would prefer them to be judged for aesthetic elegance, craft and creativity, and hope that in time they will become collector's pieces.

I served an apprenticeship as a cabinet maker, later for many years I was in charge of a workshop, designing and producing quality commissioned furniture.

In 1965 I started teaching at Brighton Polytechnic formerly College of Art, becoming responsible for all the furniture courses.

I have always felt a strong need to produce my own work. The decision to concentrate on it fully was made in 1982. Snce then I have exhibited and sold my work widely around the world.

HITCHCOCKS'

11 East Street, New Alresford SO24 9EQ (0962) 734762

10 Chapel Row, Bath BA1 1HN (0225) 330646

In 1976, Joyce Hitchcock bought the lease of a tiny shop in Market Street, Winchester. It was called 'Country Fare' and sold the paraphenalia of the seventies in a space hardly larger than a double bed. In 1980, she opened a much bigger gallery in the Regency market town of New Alresford. Here the emphasis was on contemporary crafts, work from British designers and artists of high standards and imagination. The idea grew, and in 1986 her daughter Fleur joined her in partnership and they took on a four storey house off Queen Square, Bath. Simultaneously, developers threatened the little shop in Winchester and the original 'Country Fare' was lost. It was time to change the name to 'Hitchcocks''.

The two spaces operate together, the buying is done in common, but they are also subtly different. Hitchcocks', New Alresford is a single area with a basement, it caters for a wider audience

than its daughter shop, for example, it stocks a range of handmade scale doll's house furniture, unavailable in Bath. Hitchcocks', Bath, however, has a third floor space that holds changing exhibitions and allows the gallery to show larger special pieces of work that would not normally be seen in the regular selling space. The gallery has exhibited Sarah Burnett, Janet Bolton, Alice Kettle, Jason Cleverly, Taja, Lorna Moffat, as well as many many others. There have been shows of textiles, mechanical toys, interior design, wood, painted silk, jewellery and etching.

Both galleries have continuous collections of decorative and decorated ceramics, including work by Mary Rose Young, Dart Pottery, Majolica Works, and Mark Hay. There is precious jewellery by Michael Bolton and Kevin O'Dwyer, and representative of modern media jewellery, Jane Adam and Julie Arkell. John Mainwaring and Tobias Kaye show turned and carved wood and there is studio glass from Scotland, Sark and Sussex.

Ian McKay and Tony Mann are included among makers of mechanical toys suitable for adults, whilst the work of Jim Edmiston and Opi Toys, though just as collectable, is safe for children. As well as specialising in toys, the galleries have a concentration of knitwear, from the humble arran to fabulously complicated hand knitted cardigans by top designers such as the Seatons and Muir and Osborne. To complement this, there are wide selections of hand-painted silk scarves, ties and blouses.

Although the majority of work shown is by young makers working in Britain and Ireland, the shops also stock a competitive collection of clothing from India and occasional products from developing countries.

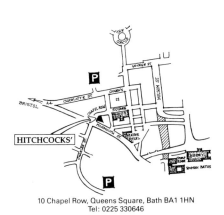

10 Chapel Row, Queens Square, Bath BA1 1HN
Tel: 0225 330646

JOHN MAINWARING

I was born in 1948 in Shropshire. I seem to have been associated with wood for most of my life. My father, who was a carpenter, had a large workshop where I used to watch, in fascination, forms being created in various hardwoods. In the mid 1970s I became involved with woodturning, making large bowls and platters, mostly out of burrs and spalted timber. I turned to sculpture mainly to add more scope to my work. There seems to be a limitless variety of ideas and forms to create.

My main interest is the creation of highly stylised animal and bird forms in a wide variety of woods. Great care is taken, in utilising the natural grain and colour of the wood, to enhance the form of the piece. Sometimes the very nature of the wood, such as the owl form pictured here, made out of driftwood, seems to dictate how the sculpture is evolved, and who can argue with Nature, the greatest artist ever?

IAN MCKAY

Trained at Buckinghamshire College of Higher Education and Hereford College of Art, Ian McKay has moved across from Ceramics and Silverwork to Furniture and Toymaking. Since summer 1991 he has been running his own workshop outside Bath and has developed several ranges of small affordable mechanical toys. The themes he has explored are: Topiary, ornamental revolving birds on ornamental bushes; The Food Chain, birds sipping nectar, birds after fishes, fishes after maggots; Nautical Calamities, from mal de mer to the Titanic.

These toys are not designed for children but provide hours of fun for discerning adults, as well as being objects of beauty. He uses home-grown woods from renewable sources, stained and decorated in luscious colours. Larger moving pieces and entertaining furniture can be made to commission, from a Deep Sea Bookcase to a Freshwater Dresser.

MARY ROSE YOUNG

Born in 1958 and based in the Forest of Dean, her pottery is not only original but beautiful. She takes ideas and designs from her surroundings — the birds, flowers and leaves of the forest — and transposes them with strong brush strokes and fresh colours onto her trademark vases, bowls, plates and cups.

Every inch of her work is painted; turn over a plate decorated with running chickens and you will find some more running around the base. This is not to say that the throwing and preparation of each piece is given any less attention. Pick up one of her cups (or better still, drink from it) and it has a crispness which somehow only a handmade ceramic item possesses.

Hailed by some as the next Clarice Cliff, and already nominated by the US Metropolitan Home as one of their 100 Designers (1990), she sells to some of the smartest stores in the world. Her work cheers you up just looking at it.

EXHIBITION OF CERAMICS

1

2

3

4

5

1. Marcio Mattos (Schomberg)
2. Marilza Gouvea (Schomberg)
3. Janet Hamer (Mid Cornwall)
4. Carolyn Genders (Gowan)
5. Ruthanne Tudball (New Ashgate)

MAKERS

7a Bath Place, Taunton, Somerset TA1 4ER (0823) 251121

Open Monday to Saturday 9am - 5.30pm

Makers is a co-operative venture established in 1984. Makers is owned and staffed by a group of west country craftsmen as an outlet for their finest work.

Every item on display is designed and made by the participating members. Each piece is either a unique one-off or one of a limited edition. Commissions are undertaken by all members.

Visit Makers where you will always find a maker on duty; and see their hand painted silk scarves and blouses, studio glass, studio and domestic pottery, turned wood, modern furniture, book binding, limited edition prints, jewellery, woven fabrics and much more.

INDEX TO PHOTOGRAPHS

MAKERS

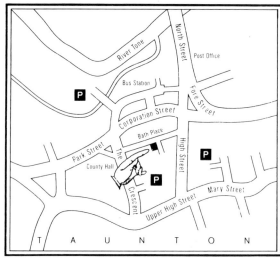

1   *Photo: Graham Cox*

2   *Photo: Studio Seventy, Langport*

3

4

6

7

9

5

8

10

MIXED EXHIBITION

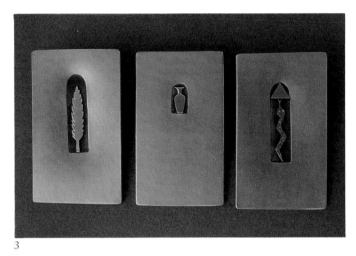

1. *Heidi Lichterman (Schomberg)*
2. *Peter Parkinson (New Ashgate)*
3. *Trevor Forrester (New Ashgate)*
4. *Ellis Palmer (Courtyard)*
5. *Glynn Thomas (Courtyard)*

MARSHALL ARTS GALLERY

3 Warland, Totnes, South Devon TQ9 5EL (0803) 863533
Open — Summer: Monday to Saturday 10am - 1pm & 2pm - 5pm except Thursday and Saturday afternoons
Winter: Tuesday, Wednesday, Friday 10am - 1pm & 2pm - 5pm and Saturday 10am - 1pm (closed Monday & Thursday)

I have always been interested in painting and crafts, but did not move to full-time work in this field until pushed by redundancy from a more mundane job when my department left the area. I began a picture framing business, working at first at home and then in a rented workshop, but increasing involvement with local painters and print-makers stirred ambitions to run a small gallery. When the moment seemed right, my wife Janet and I began hunting for combined shop, workshop and living accommodation to buy, and found what we wanted in Warland, in premises that had previously been used by a grocer, then by a glass-blower, and lastly as a toy-shop. The circle of artists and craftspeople whom we know has

expanded steadily since we bought the gallery in 1986, and searching out new people and following the developments of those we know well gives us enormous pleasure. My wife is a full-time teacher, but at weekends and in school holidays is able to share the excitement of travelling to see people and select from their work.

Most of the work shown comes from the West Country. The gallery is especially strong in studio ceramics, and also has a good variety of wood-turning, jewellery, painting and prints, and some striking and beautiful blown glass. Several exhibitions are held each year focussing on a particular craftsperson or a small group.

I feel that I am able to offer our craftspeople and visitors an atmosphere of light, peace and space in which it is possible to view and appreciate work fully. This atmosphere has been strengthened recently by extending into a third room, which has not only allowed us to put more work on display, but has improved the lighting and given a glimpse of a small courtyard garden.

Chris Marshall

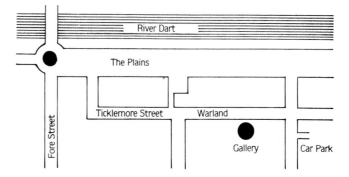

BLANDINE ANDERSON

After studying Fine Art (Ceramics), Blandine lectured at colleges in the South West of England before setting up her workshop in Devon. She now exhibits in galleries throughout Britain and is a member of the Devon Guild of Craftsmen. Her sculptural stoneware and porcelain forms are slab-built, then modelled and carved. Incised images and textures enrich the surfaces and further develop the themes. Pieces are 5cms to 75cms high (wave forms illustrated: 25cms and 15cms).

Creatures are the central element, set in a complex arrangement with other forms derived from nature. Fishes, Cetaceans and Amphibians occur frequently in these lively, often humorous compositions. Inspiration is drawn from a wide range of sources, from the habits of the creatures depicted, to ancient and modern (often oriental) artefacts. Literary allusions sometimes give further clues to the origins of the ideas. Harmonious colours are achieved through the use of slips, stoneware glazes, enamels and lustres.

NORMAN STUART CLARKE

Norman Stuart Clarke, one of Britain's leading Artist Glassblowers, works in his Studio Gallery at St Erth, Cornwall, where he can be seen creating his unique glass most days.

Since his early days at Art School, Norman has developed a distinctive 'painterly' style which decorates his glass forms. In the late seventies, in collaboration with Peter Layton, Norman developed a special iridising technique, and his mastery of this sets his work aside as highly collectable.

Pure crystal glass is melted in the furnace and coloured glass is arranged on steel benches. The hot molten glass is gathered on blowing irons from the furnace and rolled gently onto the pre- arranged coloured glass. The decorated incandescent mass is then reheated, shaped, and freely blown until Norman feels that he has coaxed the best potential form from the piece.

Norman's influences are manifold, a Cornish landscape, a pebble or a falling leaf, the power of rushing waves or the morning sun shining through a forest of pines. Norman also explores the inner spiritual world of dreams, illusions and realities.

Norman's work is exhibited worldwide, is in many prominent public and private collections, and is on permanent display at the Queen's Gallery, Buckingham Palace.

Norman's range is extensive, from exquisite vases, bottles and bowls to his monumental works of great power and beauty, all individually made and signed by the artist.

SUE HENNINGS
Enameller

Most of the jewellery I make at the moment is covered in spots and triangles — the results of my dreams and meditations. I like to think I've gained a freedom from the tight, controlled, flowery work I used to do. I specialise in champlevé enamelling, using nitric acid to etch my designs into the silver. Layers of finely ground enamel are built up in the hollows, fired in my kiln, then stoned flat. Sometimes I give the silver a high polish to match the enamel, and sometimes I leave both the silver and the enamel matt. I prefer the softer look of the matt finish.

I started enamelling 20 years ago when I was training to be an art teacher. Gradually enamelling has taken over my life. I can think of nothing better than working in my large sunny workshop in Devon, playing with pieces of silver and all the wonderful colour combinations of my enamels.

HEATHER WILLIAMS

Silver Jewellery

Heather has been a professional musician for the past 40 years and only recently has been able to devote more time and thought to her life-long interest in crafts.

Through her close connection with Dartington Hall as a pupil, student, and teacher she has been strongly influenced by such people as Kurt Jooss, Imogen Holst, Bernard and Helga Forrester, Susan Bosence and the jeweller Breon O'Casey.

In 1989 Heather began to work in silver and other metals, making rings, brooches, ear-rings and scarf-holders. The designs which Heather creates evolve as she works; a discarded metal cut-out may be enough to trigger an idea for a fantastic animal or object. Heather makes her own 'findings' which sometimes look unusual but have a simple practicality.

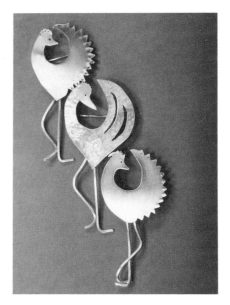

MID CORNWALL GALLERIES

Biscovey, Par, Cornwall PL24 2EG. (0726 81) 2131

Open Monday to Saturday 10am - 5pm Coffee — Ample Parking

Mid Cornwall Galleries is situated in an old school next door to St Mary's Church, to which it originally belonged. Sturdily built of local granite in the Victorian era, it has plenty of parking space in the old playground.

The Galleries were formed in these splendid premises in 1980. Visitors are pleasantly surprised by the use to which the school has been put. Well-lit exhibition areas have been created to show to perfection an abundance of fine work. On display are ceramics, glass, silks, leather, woodwork, jewellery, sculpture, as well as countless other intriguing things. Many fine paintings in water colours and oils can be seen with etchings, collages and prints, giving the overall assurance that some of the finest work in the South West is to be found here.

The Galleries present eight or nine Exhibitions a year; this adds to the general delight of the regular vistors who find something different each time they call. Members of the Craftsmen Potters Association and the Royal Institute of Painters in Water Colours are among some of the more prestigious exhibitors, many of them being regular contributors throughout the year.

All in all, a visit here is quite an experience and a moment of respite from such a wonderful assault on the senses can be had over a cup of freshly brewed coffee.

We are on the A390 3 miles East of St Austell at St Blazey There is a regular bus service from St Austell station to our door. We look forward to your company.

We Are At Biscovey

JANET HAMER
Ceramics

I am fascinated by the high-temperature ceramic process and its potential for creative expression. I aim to use a potter's making methods and to exploit colours and glazes, linking them with a subject — often a lively aquatic bird. I am particularly interested in Grebes, Mandarins, and shore-line birds.

There are many rich possibilities — opportunities for the development of the raw material throughout its shaping, and the changes wrought by the chemistry of glazing and firing. The creation of each bird springs from the meeting point of a ceramic statement with the observation of a fascinating creature. That point comes when I see that particular clay shapes and fired colours can be used in an authentic potter's way that will link with a vital characteristic of the bird. I use glazes to evoke either the naturalistic colouring of a bird, or to express an emotive response. The glaze must retain its own identity of colour, translucency or texture.

JILL HOLLAND

Here I am celebrating my 38th birthday, a woman of my times. Many pots have been made now, lots of experiments, some beginning to get there... just beginning. Colours, shapes, patterns, Matisse, Cuagan, Miro, Klee, all uplift, inspire, are joyful, light and mysterious.

Look at those colours and forms, don't they thrill you! To make is joyful. So many choices. A wiggle here, a dash there, a light touch, a bold touch, warm orange, cool green, sharp yellow, stars, fruit, moons and flowers. The mystery of pots thrown on the wheel or of huge sheets of soft folding clay moulded into a bowl, a dish, a saucerful of secrets. The mystery of fire, even in an electric kiln. All is magic for the pot maker.

LYN MUIR

Born in East Anglia, Lyn Muir studied at Colchester School of Art from where she gained her NDD in Illustration. After leaving college she worked in theatrical design.

She moved to Cornwall in the mid seventies with her family, from where she set up her workshop.

Combining her interest and skills working in the 3-dimensional and her graphics training, she began working primarily on her wooden figures. Most of her work is purely decorative, while other pieces, such as the 'Jumping Clown' shown in the photograph, are incorporated into boxes. This particular piece stands 8" high and, like most of her work, is made from pine and painted in acrylics with a polished finish.

Her characters represent people from every walk of life, usually with humorous appeal. Lyn is particularly interested in bathers and country folk, therefore the location of her home on the North Cornwall coast provides much inspiration. This has developed into a fascination with Edwardian style and 1920s bathers which feature prominently in her work, using old photographs from her large collection for inspiration and research. She has taken the Edwardian beach scene further with, for example, triptychs of bathing huts with bathers to make them feel 'more at home'.

Lyn also works in the 2-dimensional with her greeting cards with hand-painted designs on 4ml birch-ply. Once again, they depict many different characters, from country folk, bathers, businessmen, sportsmen, Adams, Eves, and many more.

Lyn sells through galleries and also does private commission work throughout the UK and America. She is a member of the British Toymakers Guild, Cornwall Crafts Association, and Devon Guild of Craftsmen.

SUZIE MARSH
Ceramic Sculpture

Suzie gained her degree in Ceramic Sculpture at Exeter College of Art. Leaving college in 1982 she spent several years as a designer for Devon-based companies where she gained an insight into the industrial production of ceramics. In 1987, prompted by a commission for a museum in Taiwan, she established her own workshop in order to concentrate full-time on her own sculpture.

Suzie's work reflects her fascination with the animal form, particularly cats and birds, and her inspiration is drawn from drawings, photographs, videos, and the animals which surround the Devon farmhouse where she lives with her own cats. Each piece is hand-built in stoneware clay and fired to 1280 degrees. Glazes are used sparingly, as Suzie feels that they obscure too much of the sculpture's form and movement. Instead she prefers to use oxides to heighten the colour and depth of the clay and restricts glazing to the small decorative highlights of more ornate pieces. Being high-fired, the sculptures are suitable for use in the house or garden.

DELAN COOKSON
Thrown Porcelain

I work on my own, throwing individual bottles or container forms in porcelain, aiming for that elusive special form with its satisfying completeness that I see in museums. The attraction of porcelain for me is its smooth whiteness, which reflects all the brilliance of my coloured glazes.

I am chiefly concerned with exploring thrown forms, each pot is individual, or a variation on a theme. I am very aware that the pot is a hollow vessel whose internal volume can be expressed in many ways, that the external character or shape is the result of line, proportion, balance, or even the form of a lip. The accent of a curve can determine whether a shape is invested with a breath of vitality. This kind of tension can be seen for example in my cylinder bottles which are thrown in two sections, the vertical form being brought crisply to a finish with the flat top emphasising the taut volume of the form.

YERJA

Ceramics by Chris Speyer, Textiles by Kath Ukleja

Yerja Ceramics and Textiles is the partnership of studio potter Chris Speyer and textile painter Kath Ukleja. Yerja's workshops are situated in the picturesque town of Bampton in Devon.

Kath Ukleja paints wallhangings, bedspreads, curtain fabrics, cushions and clothing — each piece an individual painting, her sunny Mediterranean colours dancing across crisp cottons and linens or shimmering silk. New for 1991 — The Transatlantic Collection — all silk fashionwear, created in collaboration with Californian designer/ maker Sally Babson.

Chris Speyer's one-off thrown and handpressed plates and platters, his 'bird boats' and 'serving fishes' are alive with colour and crawling with creatures. He also produces a range of decorative domestic pottery, available in three patterns, 'Bird', 'Fish' and 'Melon. All work is oxidisation fired stoneware.

FRANK HAMER

Plates and Dishes

Frank Hamer loves the countryside which has influenced his ceramics. He now concentrates on graphic images taken from nature. Typical is this fish dish. Other popular images are flowers and fruit, and landscapes including buildings, ships and harbours.

The imagery always starts with observations of actual objects, but challenges arise as the image, composition, ceramic materials and techniques are combined. The final work is created in the fire. The result is simply a dialogue between artist and materials: the artist directing the image; the materials making their own unique contribution to the artistic statements.

His work consists entirely of decorative plates and dishes in reduced stoneware. These have integral hangers for wall display and are also used for serving food. The pieces should be read on four levels: as plates or dishes; as overall decorative objects; as specific imagery and as ceramic happenings.

LAURENCE MCGOWAN

Born in Salisbury in 1942, Laurence McGowan, after an earlier career in surveying, returned to his native Wiltshire in 1979 to establish his own workshop, having spent several years working with Alan Caiger-Smith at Aldermaston Pottery. Trained in the traditional majolica technique of pottery painting, McGowan now applies this knowledge to enhance his thrown stoneware forms with ever-changing brushwork patterns distilled from plant and animal forms. Whilst in no way imitative, these often contain echoes of his interest in the decorative arts of the Middle East and their assimilation into the contemporary vocabulary through the Arts and Craft Movement. Some pots are also inscribed, exploring the extra dimension calligraphy can give to a piece.

Commissioned presentation pieces form much of his output, many of which go to the United States where regular exhibitions of his work are also held.

McGowan's work is represented in many collections, both private and public, and is used and enjoyed in many homes around the world. He is a Fellow of the Craft Potters Association.

PAUL JACKSON

Ceramics and Domestic Ware

Paul began his training in the early 1970s, working part-time with Joanna Constantinidis. He went on to study full-time at Harrow School of Art, qualifying in 1977, followed by a period as pottery supervisor in a South London job creation scheme. During the two years he was there, Paul became senior supervisor of all the craft departments, and began to develop his own ideas for the form and decoration of domestic ware.

In 1979 he moved to Cornwall and established the Helland Pottery, where he was able to develop and refine his characteristic approach to brightly decorated earthenware, based initially on French and Italian ideas. Later, he found himself drawn to forms and decoration from all over the world, including Russian graphic and Islamic styles.

In due course, this eclectic attitude led to a re-appraisal of the traditional potter's role, experimentation with painterly techniques such as life drawing, and the incorporation of both abstract and figurative images.

His most recent ceramics have a semi-literary flavour, acting almost as a visual diary of the potter's life.

MONTPELLIER GALLERY

27 The Courtyard, Montpellier Street, Cheltenham, Glos, GL50 1SR. Telephone & Fax (0242) 515165

Open Monday to Saturday 9.30 am - 5.30 pm throughout the year

Montpellier Gallery opened in April 1990 after a long quest for the right setting in which to display the finest of contemporary fine art and craft where different media could be seen to their best advantage. We have found a unique setting for the Gallery, in Cheltenham's Montpellier, where some of Britain's finest Regency terraces line elegant streets bedecked with flowers. The Courtyard, where the Gallery is located, has a delightful continental atmosphere, with outdoor cafes and balconied shops, a special feature in keeping with the flavour of Cheltenham's exceptional architecture.

It was surprising to find that Cheltenham had no existing galleries showing contemporary crafts to this extent, combined with pictures, on a substantial scale. The response to Montpellier Gallery has been tremendous — this was obviously a gap that needed to be filled, and such has been the success that we were encouraged to open a second gallery in December 1991 in Stratford-upon-Avon.

The Gallery offers a light and spacious environment for the display of studio ceramics and glass, together with designer jewellery, by new and established craftspeople, alongside

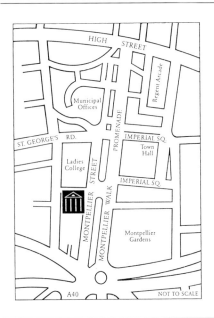

paintings in oil and watercolour, and a comprehensive range of contemporary printmaking — etching, engraving and silkscreens.

There is an exhibition in the Gallery every other month, either solo exhibitons or work by various artists brought together around a theme. We also specialise in featuring artists and craftspeople whose works complement each other in colour, texture and inspiration. In between exhibitions, we display a selection of work in different media, representing a variety of artists.

We have recently forged a most worthwhile link with a gallery in Normandy, one of the leading contemporary galleries north of Paris, with whom we have regular exchanges of work, thus promoting the finest quality work by British artists in a European market.

With over ten years experience in the world of art and marketing, proprietor Linda Burridge, a graduate of Art History, can offer considerable knowledge to customers. The Galleries are run jointly with her husband, Peter Burridge, a leading artist- printmaker in his own right.

A newsletter detailing exhibitions and events is published twice yearly and is available upon application.

ROBERT WHELPTON

Robert Whelpton was born in 1952 in Hartlepool. He attended North Staffordshire Polytechnic, studying ceramics, and on leaving in 1974, spent several years abroad.

After the break from working in ceramics, Rob felt the need to return to working with clay, which prompted his return to England in 1983 as a trainee at Dartington Pottery. After two years, he moved to Wiltshire and established Krukker Ceramics with his wife Vicky, who produces her own range of porcelain. The present workshop was set up in 1989.

Rob's pottery is raku fired, a technique in which the red-hot pot is removed from the kiln with tongs when the glaze has melted, and is covered with sawdust. This results in the lustre and crackle glaze effects and the blackening of unglazed areas which is characteristic of the raku process.

All Rob's pots are made on the wheel and decorated using bird, animal and fish motifs, which are either incised onto the surface or pierced through the pot's wall. These are in rhythmic intertwined shapes, with much beauty and a certain humour. They are coloured using a combination of coloured slips and metallic salts.

Rob's work is collected throughout Britain, and he is a member of the Devon Guild of Craftsmen.

LOUISE PARRY

Louise Parry was born in 1965. She studied jewellery at Birmingham Polytechnic, graduating in 1987. Louise set up her own workshop in Gloucestershire, from where she creates her highly imaginative jewellery.

She specialises in pieces made from ceramics, silver and brass combined in intricate, often quirky designs, decorated with patterns of stars and scrolls making them 'sparkle'. She enjoys the combination of metal and colour — lapis lazuli with gold, blue resin with brass. There is also a strong Masai influence in some of the motifs, using triangular shapes, which work well in adorning the body.

Her jewellery shows great spontaneity, from the freedom she feels using flexible materials. Louise's jewellery appeals to all ages, such is the enjoyment with which she creates it, which is clearly expressed.

PETER BURRIDGE

Peter Burridge graduated with a BA (Hons) in 3D Design from the School of Jewellery and Silversmithing, Birmingham, in 1981. He was introduced to the techniques of printmaking during an R.S.A. bursary study tour to Italy in 1982, one of many awards he received for his jewellery and silver designs.

On his return to Britain he established a workshop to develop the techniques of etching, specialising in 'Soft Ground', a process which gives a gentle, crayon-like texture, perfect for the atmospheric courtyard and garden scenes he portrays.

Now well represented in the USA, Hong Kong, Australia, and Europe, he also exhibits regularly at the R.A. Summer Show and in many of Britain's galleries. He currently works in Gloucestershire, alongside his wife Linda Burridge, running two Galleries and his printmaking workshop.

MONTPELLIER GALLERY

8 Chapel Street, Stratford-upon-Avon, Warwickshire, CV37 3EP Telephone & Fax (0789) 261161

Open Monday to Saturday, 9.30 am - 5.30 pm throughout the year.

Montpellier Gallery opened in Stratford-upon-Avon in December 1991, based on the success of the Gallery running in Cheltenham since April 1990. In the difficult climate at this time, the deciding factor in launching a second venture was that this was a most marvellous opportunity presenting itself — a long term vision!

There was a gallery here which had been established for 25 years, by one of Britain's leading craft dealers, Peter Dingley, whose world-wide acclaim reflects his uncompromising standards of excellence in ceramics and glass. The tradition and expectations he had built up would be difficult to follow, but loyal customers and visitors to the gallery bring a ready responsiveness and enthusiasm for the crafts with them. Although we have introduced a completely new stock, many of the potters and glassmakers represented by our predecessor have also been stocked at our Cheltenham gallery over the years, and this has ensured a most satisfying continuity at Stratford. Beyond this, we have introduced designer jewellery, contemporary paintings and printmaking techniques as new elements alongside the crafts already established here.

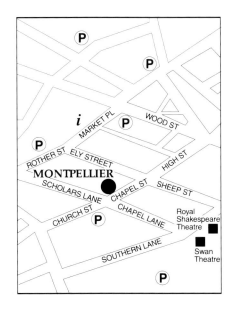

Set in a 400 year old building in the heart of Shakepeare's Stratford, the Gallery comprises three adjoining rooms, opening to a delightful tiny courtyard which floods the rooms with natural light — a precious commodity!

The Gallery has a programme of exhibitions held every other month, featuring individual artists and craftspeople, or work brought together around a theme, whilst between exhibitions the varied displays represent a selection of the finest studio ceramics, glass and designer jewellery, alongside paintings and etchings by new and established artists.

A newsletter detailing exhibitions and events is published twice yearly and is available on application.

Montpellier Gallery's proprietor graduated as an Art Historian, pursued qualifications in the decorative arts, and is currently continuing post-graduate research in British Art History. With over ten years experience in the world of art and marketing, considerable knowledge and experience are offered to customers. The Gallery is run jointly with her husband, Peter Burridge, a leading artist-printmaker in his own right.

Linda Burridge

MALCOLM SUTCLIFFE

Malcolm Sutcliffe was born in 1954 and studied ceramics and glass at Birmingham Polytechnic. He set up his first workshop on leaving Polytechnic in Worcestershire, where he also taught.

After working with other glassmakers for some time, Malcolm has once again set up his own studio, in Derbyshire, where he now works with the assistance of his wife.

Malcolm enjoys making bowls, dishes and plates which have clean, smooth, simple shapes offering a surface similar to that of a canvas on which the images can be sandblasted. At present he is working on the watery theme of 'Dolphins' and 'Whales'. The dolphins can be seen leaping and diving through the surf around the bowls. His latest work goes beneath the waves and submerges into the deep blue sea with the Humpback Whales.

Malcolm's glass is collected throughout Britain, Europe and the USA and Japan, and is represented in major collections in museusms and art galleries.

SUSAN MATHER

After graduating in Three-Dimensional Design — studying wood, metal, ceramics and glass — from Manchester Polytechnic, Susan worked for four years as a Graphic Designer. She then started her first workshop.

Her early work was in wood, producing carved and turned jewellery. Simple experiments making rolled beads from paper led to her developing a 'folding' technique which has resulted in a range of exquisite pleated jewellery, in spiral and fan shapes.

Each piece of work is richly coloured in a multitude of patterns and colour combinations before being lacquered many times to produce a finish that is water-resistant and strong. Often the jewellery incorporates semi-precious stones, twisted coils of gold or silver wire or metal spirals.

In 1991, Susan moved to Staffordshire where she now works in partnership with her brother Christopher, a cabinet maker. As well as producing the lacquered paper jewellery, she is also involved in the production of decorative furniture.

HILARY LAFORCE

Hilary Laforce studied ceramics at West Surrey College of Art and Design, graduating in 1981. After travelling in France and Canada, she started her own workshop in 1985.

Her forms are inspired by the ancient Greek and Roman ceramics, especially in the use of terracotta and its effects. More recently, the traditions of South and Central America have also influenced her work. Many pieces seem to have a balance of their own, on slender bases offering dynamic lines to the classical shapes. Hilary uses coils of clay, pinched to paper fineness, for her pots, which are glazed with metal lustres applied to the surface of the smooth terracotta, creating unusual textures. More recently, she has added gold and bronze to the vibrant blues and purples and subtle chalky colours. Many pieces take on the look of being patinated, bringing them even closer to the unearthed aspect of their ancestors.

Hilary Laforce is one of Britain's leading ceramists, and her work is widely represented in Britain and abroad.

THE NEW ASHGATE GALLERY

Wagon Yard, Farnham, Surrey GU9 7PS (0252) 713208

Open Tuesday to Saturday 10am - 1.30pm, 2.30pm - 5pm

The New Ashgate Gallery is housed in a 17th century building situated in the centre of the pleasant country town of Farnham on the Surrey/Hampshire border, an hour from London—by rail from Waterloo, or by road via the A3.

The gallery, established in 1976, includes an area to display and sell a wide range of work by leading contemporary craftspeople, in addition to the regularly changing exhibitions of paintings and sculpture, and upstairs Ruta Brown has her jewellery workshop.

The policy of the New Ashgate Gallery is to show the work of established professional artists and craftspeople with equal emphasis, and to afford exhibition opportunities to young people at the outset of their careers.

Commissions can be arranged, and the gallery is recommended by the Crafts Council of Great Britain.

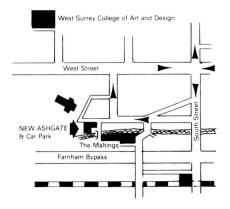

PETER PARKINSON

Having studied at the Royal College of Art and worked initially as an Industrial Designer, I became involved with Artist Blacksmithing in the late seventies. Since then I have designed and made a wide variety of work, essentially forged in mild steel, but occasionally including other metals such as copper, brasses, stainless steels and titanium.

My time is divided between the making of speculative work — candleholders, clocks, mirrors, sundials — and larger commissioned pieces of public art or architectural metalwork. These have included: forged steel window grilles for the Crafts Gallery of Portsmouth City Museum; an 11m entrance archway for a new pedestrian scheme in Ivegate, Bradford, Yorkshire; a hanging mobile in patinated metals in the Russell-Cotes Museum, Bournemouth; forged steel and patinated brass Terrestrial and Celestial Globes for the Commonwealth Development Office, London (see photograph); and a steel and cast bronze triumphal gateway in London Street, Basingstoke.

I enjoy the plastic working of hot metal under the hammer, each blow making its mark literally in the heat of the moment. I also enjoy the challenge of designing and planning each piece. It is this combination of intellectual and physical effort, a mixture of deliberation and spontaneity, which for me holds the magic.

In parallel with this, producing speculative work for sale through the gallery allows me freedom to develop ideas for their own sake, while commissioned work demands a more formal discipline in responding to the particular needs of the site and the client.

I have exhibited widely in Britain and also in Germany and America

MIKE SCOTT (Chai)

I am currently involved in making lathe-turned wooden vessels, wallpieces and sculpture, exploiting the possibilities of form, texture, colour, natural features, burning and scorching, warpage and shrinkage, in order to produce individual pieces with a strong presence.

My own visual references are many; African and other tribal artefacts, archaeological ruins such as amphitheatres, landscape and natural forms, ritual and ceremonial vessels, all contribute to my personal iconography. I like to incorporate other materials such as rope, leather, metals, wire and cord. My pieces range in scale from small pots to large pieces of over 36" diameter.

I use native hardwoods, mostly elm and oak burrs, the grain pattern and textured surface of the burr being particularly suited to creating images of landscape, or in the case of my raw sand-blasted pieces, evoking the erosion of time.

My pieces generally evolve on the lathe during the making process, as the different qualities of each block of wood will demand a different response, allowing me to use my intuition and imagination to create pieces that express my own personal vision.

Photo: Michel Focard

RUTHANNE TUDBALL

Sodium Glazed Stoneware

All of my work is raw glazed, slip decorated, and once-fired sodium glazed stoneware. My main concern is with the clay and the pleasure of manipulating it during throwing. I want to make forms that capture the soft plasticity of the material and the energy of the making process, and which have both dignity and a lively freshness. Sodium glazing can have dramatic effects on the surface of the pots, emphasising the making process and path of the flame across the work, rendering each pot unique. I try to obtain a glaze quality and colour response similar to salt glazing, but with sodium compounds other than salt to eliminate the pollution of chlorine gas. I make my pots to be lived with, handled, and used.

Born in California, USA, I received a Post-graduate Diploma in Ceramics from Goldsmiths' College after years of being mainly self-taught and after gaining an Honours degree in English and a Post-graduate Certificate in Education. I am a Fellow and Council Member of the Craft Potters' Association of Great Britain.

TREVOR FORRESTER

Born in 1960 in Toronto, Canada, Trevor graduated from Camberwell School of Arts and Crafts in the mid-eighties.

Inspiration for his jewellery and metal pieces comes from many sources — music, films, cartoons, geographical locations, children's toys and games, animals and birds. He uses pewter with other metals such as brass, silver and gold. The brooches and ear-rings stem from his view of the world as a stage with snapshot views representing particular events.

Thus the low-relief backgrounds act as a frame or canvas upon which images appear, creating lively and often humorous pieces of jewellery. To Trevor, humour plays an important role, as can be seen in the brooch illustrated here, entitled 'The Dare'. He feels that pewter is generally an undervalued metal for jewellery, but he is altering this by bringing it to a wider audience at an affordable price. Trevor's jewellery can be found in galleries throughout England, Scotland, Wales and abroad.

JAYNE BARBER
Metalsmith

Born in 1963, I studied at the Sir John Cass School of Art in London, where I took a degree in Jewellery and Silversmithing. By the time that I had completed my studies, I was hooked on the traditional techniques of the silversmith, but I wished to use them in a more sculptural way. I enjoy working with the more flexible and less precious metal alloys of copper. This gives me the freedom to be more adventurous.

My work consists of vessels/pots and bowls. My pieces are handmade and are all one-offs. I work mainly in gilding metal and brass and use a variety of finishes. I mostly patina my work, which is the chemical colouration of metals, and I also use gold and silver leaf.

My forms relate to natural shapes, seeds and plants, and I am beginning to realise that they mainly derive from the fossils, shells and rocks that I had around me as a child (my father is a geologist). I have exhibited in a number of galleries around the country.

RUTA BROWN

The use of reticulation first occurred in Czarist Russia, where the process of heating flat sheet metal to produce a surface texture was used by Fabergé and other goldsmiths, who termed it 'samorodok', literally meaning 'born by itself'. The texture is self-created, requiring nothing but the application of heat. From there it spread to Scandinavia, where it is still used for objects such as cigarette boxes.

I am currently exploiting another creative use to which this technique can be put — the reticulation of an entire finished piece, or completed unit parts, of jewellery, fabricated from sheet silver and 18 carat gold. Pieces are first forged into shape, then subjected to fusing temperature to create wrinkled textures, varying in appearance from delicate silk to ancient leather. Care is necessary, as overheating can easily cause the three-dimensional work to collapse.

It is this element of risk and unpredictability of both structure and texture which ensures that each piece is unique.

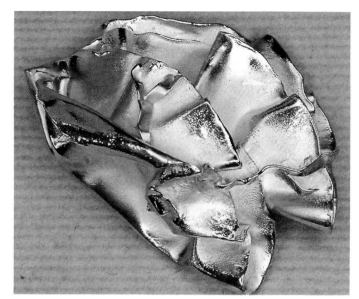

EXHIBITION OF CERAMICS

1

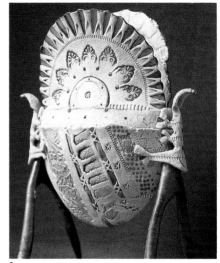

2

3

4

1. Pauline Zelinski (Alpha)
2. Pam Schomberg (Schomberg)
3. Mary Rose Young (Hitchcock)
4. Frank Hamer (Mid Cornwall)
5. Sue Ford (Alpha)

5

PAM SCHOMBERG GALLERY

12 St Johns Street, Colchester, Essex CO2 7AN (0206) 769458 (day) (0206) 564624 (evening)

Open Monday to Saturday 10.30am - 5pm, closed Thursday

The Gallery is situated at a busy location in the centre of Colchester and has become established as an independent collection promoting a distinctive variety of the best in contemporary applied art and craftsmanship. It aims to stimulate interest amongst local corporate and public institutions and forms exhibitions towards architects and interior designers as well as the main job of introducing the craftsman's work to the art buying community, and broadening its accessibility to a still wider audience. All the work is of the highest standard, selected for its quality and individuality. We have felt privileged that some of the leading national artists have accepted our invitation to show their work.

As a potter herself, with a studio below the Gallery, Pam has a natural interest in ceramics which probably forms the backbone to the collection. There have been major exhibitions by such well known makers as Robin Welch, Jane Perryman, Ruth Dupré and Jeremy James. However, woven textiles by such artists as Peter Collingwood and Kathleen McFarlane usually adorn the walls, together with painted and appliqué silk. Turned and carved wood by Bert Marsh, Mike Scott and Guy Taplin has also been successfully exhibited together with wooden toys, studio glass and metalwork. There is always a good selection of unique contemporary jewellery.

Since being opened by the Mayor on 30th June 1991 the Gallery has

been met with much enthusiasm and has made many friends. There have been eight very successful exhibitions to date, showing the wide variety of work mentioned earlier, a quarterly 'Gallery Review' newsletter has been circulated, and we hope to have more of the evening lectures that guests found very rewarding.

The premises still has its original 30's facade, and besides the street level where changing exhibitions are staged, there is an upper gallery which holds a body of work and operates more on the shop principle. We hope to create a friendly welcoming atmosphere for artist and patron alike and encourage visitors to become uninhibited in their attitude to the work as an art form. There are still many people who do not normally visit galleries and have never considered buying any form of art. It is always a pleasure to cross this boundary and give them an insight into a world many of us take for granted.

The Gallery has a strong sense of working with the artist craftsman. After all it is run by an artist for artists and grows in supporting the artists by selling their work.

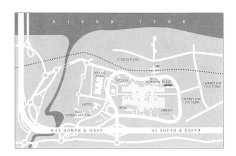

HEIDI LICHTERMAN
Weaver

Born in 1941 in the USA, Heidi studied Landscape Architecture at Harvard before going on to run nature programmes including some on television. Both areas of interest have been amalgamated in her weaving. Her wall hangings are strongly influenced by and influence their surroundings (some hangings are 30 feet high). She enjoys the challenge of making a piece which is appropriate to the site. Her work is largely abstract, based on her intimate knowledge of the natural world.

Already established in leading craft galleries in America, she moved to England in 1981 and has her studio near Cambridge. She uses ikat (wrapping and tying the yarn before dyeing) and dip-dyeing techniques for her weaving in silk. She has exhibited internationally, and her work is in major corporate collections around the world including Tokyo, Singapore, Jakarta, Hong Kong, from New York to Los Angeles, and in many locations in England. She is a Fellow of the Society of Designer-Craftsmen and a member of the Cambridge Society of Painters and Sculptors.

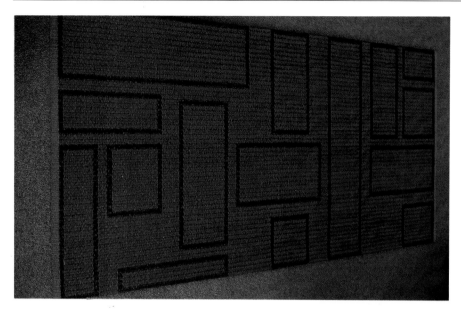

JASON COLLINGWOOD

Flat-woven reversible rugs very strongly woven in wool, horsehair or mohair on a linen warp. Sizes vary from the average of 2m x 1m to much larger pieces which are woven in strips and then sewn together, the biggest rug to date being 4m x 3m.

The rugs are woven using the Shaft Switching technique which enables the weaver to alter the threading while weaving the rug. This means that complex designs can be woven much faster than by using traditional methods. Although the rugs are meant for the floor they have been used as wall hangings.

Though most of the work has been sold to private houses both here and in the States, commissions include a large hanging for offices in central London and a series of rugs for a castle in Switzerland. The work has been exhibited widely throughout the UK and for the past four years has been on show at the Chelsea Craft Fair. Foreign shows include a one-man exhibition in Amsterdam and various mixed shows in America. In addition to this, in 1991 the Tate Gallery purchased a rug for their Contemporary Art Society collection. At present there are over 60 designs which can be repeated in any two colourways. The rugs can either be finished with tassels or with a straight woven edge. Wholesale prices start at around £115 for a 1 x 1 m. rug.

JOHN CHIPPERFIELD

Ceramics and Glass

Graduating in ceramics from the Central School of Art and Design, London in 1966, John Chipperfield has designed and manufactured a wide range of tableware and other functional ceramics over many years.

From the early 1980s however, this has increasingly given way to the making of vessels (predominantly jugs and dishes) of a more expressive and less utilitarian nature (see photograph of a jug).

Since 1984 he has additionally produced kiln-formed glass — usually in the form of dishes with iridescent polychrome designs. (See illustration).

Working with and exhibiting both materials in parallel enables him to exploit the similarities whilst emphasising the differences between them.

The influences on his work are extremely diverse — from wildlife, ancient middle eastern ceramics and Romanesque Tuscan architecture to stimuli produced by music and many aspects of contemporary art and design.

A member of the Suffolk Craft Society, East Anglian Potters Association, and Norfolk Contemporary Craft Society, his work has been widely exhibited and is in collections throughout the world.

HAYLEY SMITH

After travelling and studying part-time in the USA, I returned to Cardiff where I resumed my training, graduating in 1991 with a BA (Hons) Degree in Art Education. It was during my degree course that I first encountered wood turning (1989) leading to my specialisation in it.

I make bangles, platters and bowls, turned on the lathe from native hard woods e.g. beech, elm, sycamore. The forms of my platters and bowls are refined, and some of the following elements have been introduced as embellishment, either one or a combination of: silver wire, colour (pigments, bleaching, scorching) and texture (incising, inscribing, wirebrushing).

By contrast the bangles are large and bold. Unlike the platters and bowls, they have a raw quality, the woods' features e.g. bark pockets and splits, are fully exploited. Most bangles are turned 'green' (unseasoned), some are microwaved to accelerate the drying process, which creates a textured surface that can be exploited further by embellishment.   *Photo: Michel Focard*

PETER COLLINGWOOD

Peter Collingwood weaves wall-hangings in a unique technique invented by him 30 years ago. The materials used are Swedish linen, usually black and natural but they can be in colour, plus stainless steel rods. Hangings can be flat or 3-D and vary in size from 20-40cm in width and can be of any length. To date there are over 220 designs, all of which can be repeated exactly. Each hanging carries a small metal label with the design number and my signature on it. The hangings, called Macrogauzes, can be hung flat against a wall or window or be free hanging.

Though the majority have gone into private houses, large ones have been woven (in sections) for offices, banks and embassies — the latest such is in the Queen Elizabeth Conference Centre, Westminster.

Several have been purchased by museums such as the Victoria and Albert and the Sainsbury Collection and in similar places world-wide. Their biggest display was in the exhibition of 1969 at the V and A, with the potter Hans Coper, the first time that the work of any living craftsman had been shown there. Other one-person shows have been held in Japan, Australia, Denmark, Norway, Holland, USA.

Peter Collingwood received the OBE in 1974, the first handweaver to get it, and the Worshipful Company of Weavers Prize Scheme Medal in 1989.

Peter Collingwood has written five standard books on textile techniques and regularly conducts workshops, usually on rug weaving, in America.

No catalogue of designs is available, but a selection of slides can be lent. Prices start at around £50 wholesale.

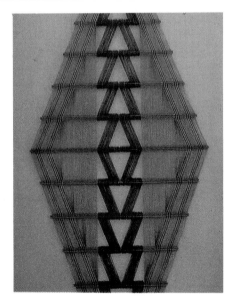

MIKE GODDARD
Potter

Born in 1942, Mike Goddard first trained as an architect and then found ceramics. He trained at Harrow Art School under Mick Casson and Victor Margpie.

Repetition throwing played a large part in his training and he still loves the discipline of this skill. Mike spends his time between his workshop in France and the workshop in Manningtree. Both workshops produce a large range of functional domestic stoneware and a range of traditional gardenware.

The architectural background has influenced his 'one-off' pots, which are a range of ceramic clocks, often using architectural features, brackets, finials and window features and pots on stands with rolled handles.

All the pots are fired in a 30 cu ft gas kiln, the frost proof gardenware to 1120°C and the reduced stoneware to 1300°C. Mike is currently making large bottles and jugs thrown and altered with decorative pressed handles and glazed in a range of dry glazes

MARIANNE SQUAIR
Designer Jeweller

After graduating from Sir John Cass in 1988 with a BA Hons. in jewellery and silversmithing, I developed the theme in my jewellery of forms and illusions created by frozen liquids and ice. By the use of contrasting texture, colour and materials I aim to create a fluid image that produces the dramatic yet delicate effect of fusion between ice and metal.

By exploiting their natural reaction to heat, I encompass acrylic with silver and 24ct. gold plate to create delicate amulets that entwine around the arm, rings that twist around the finger and earrings that swirl over the ear. Colour is used to emphasise form, enhance contrast and create depth.

Tactility and wearability play an important part in all my designs. A piece of jewellery should be a pleasure to touch as well as to wear. As each piece is individually designed and made, no two pieces are identical. Thus it is aimed at a customer to whom lasting quality and originality are equally important as owning a piece of fashionable, collectable jewellery.

DAVID WALTERS
The Particular Pottery

I was born and brought up in Natal, South Africa and came to live in Kenninghall, Norfolk in 1988. The thrust of my involvement with pots stems from a strong (colonial!) independence and a wish to make my own way, and kick my own bum when things go wrong! A University Fine Arts Degree with majors in Ceramics and History of Art, has enabled me to develop the skills to pursue a pragmatic career, purposely making accessible objects in form, function and price. This approach has resulted in a good living for over twenty years and a thoroughly enjoyable working life. Currently using only porcelain (Harry Frazer) my range includes large urns and platters (pictured) and all sizes of decorated reduction fired bowls. My studio is a peaceful restored Particular Baptist Chapel and in the upstairs gallery we sell directly to the public, seven days a week, a fair collection of my thrown ware. I even (reluctantly) take orders for purpose made dinner services.

DAVID ROBERT CARTER
Contemporary metalwork

It all started, as they say, with a poem, written to 'tart up' the cover page of my final year microbiology thesis in 1984. It ignited in me something that the previous years of study had failed to do, and I knew instantly that I wanted to do something creative, but did not know what.

After graduating I drifted about experimenting with various arts, before becoming 'fired with iron' in 1986, and setting up my first workshop. Unfortunately I did not have any practical experience and so decided the best way to learn about the medium was to work in engineering, starting at the very bottom, and working up to become a skilled industrial metalworker. I now have a large studio forge near Wisbech.

I enjoy the feeling of doing battle with the metal, using both ancient methods and the latest technology, and like the robust nature of the material, giving a sense of longevity to the end result. This is very handy if you are as clumsy as I am!

Photo: James Austin

MARILZA GOUVEA
Ceramics

Born in Brazil, where there was little opportunity to study ceramics, I came to England in the early '70s. I started studying ceramics at the Richmond Institute with Anita Hoy and subsequently completed a Diploma Course in Ceramics at Goldsmith College, London, in 1984.

In my studio I work mainly in stoneware and 'T' material using a variety of decorative techniques, my final work being reduction fired at 1260°C.

My approach to decoration is intuitive using patterns and movements to express myself like a musician or a dancer would. Music and dance are the main influences in my work. Indeed, musical improvisation and my early memories of the joyful and colourful atmosphere of Carnival in Rio, continue to exert a strong influence upon my work.

Having been trained as a psychologist and having a keen interest in anthropology, I am inspired and interested in ancient and simple societies where everyday hand-made objects assume an importance in people's lives not found in more modern cultures. By travelling extensively in my own country and also abroad as far as India and Japan I was able to enrich and reassure these feelings.

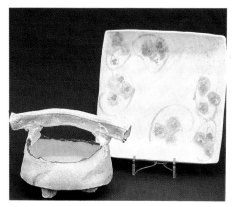

MARCIO MATTOS
Ceramics

Born in Rio de Janeiro, Brazil. Arrived in Europe in the early seventies as a professional musician working in the areas of Jazz, Modern Dance and Contemporary Music. Trained at Goldsmith College, Diploma in Art and Design, Ceramics. In 1987 participated in the international Ceramics Workshop, Tokoname, Japan. Works in own Ceramics Studio with Marilza Gouvea in North London. An active member of the London Potters Association, has exhibited, lectured and held workshops in Britain, Brazil and Japan.

Works mainly in red stoneware and 'T' Material, gas fired. Pieces are entirely hand-built, inspired by geological marks and ancient man-made artefacts. As in music, the creative process of Free Improvisation is important to the work. Work in private and public collections in Britain, France, Germany, Japan, USA, Brazil and Lebanon.

ROBERT CROOKS
First Glass

In 1986 Robert Crooks took the opportunity to work at The Glasshouse, Covent Garden, London, under the masterful eye of one of the last working craftsmen from the great Whitefriars glass factory. Since then he has not looked back, gaining an ever increasing reputation for being one of the best and still one of the youngest glassmakers and designers in the country.

In 1990 Robert set up his *First Glass* workshop in Gloucestershire. He set himself certain ideals and goals. The thinking behind his production glassware of goblets, decanters, candlesticks and so on was that 'the glass should be well designed and, very importantly, it should be made to the highest standard of craftsmanship. At the same time it should be functional for all occasions and essentially as distanced from factory made glassware as possible'. By introducing glassware which is colourful, adventurous and often witty, and at the same time accessible to as many people as possible, his aim has been to increase an awareness to the alternative to traditional cut-crystal glassware which has been predominant for too long.

Alongside the production ware, his One-Off pieces and Limited Editions provide the opportunity for experiment and innovation. From decorative semi-functional pieces, including contemporary chandeliers and mirrors, to a wider range of interior fittings, the challenge of stretching to the limits his skill as a maker and the limits of the glass itself never ceases to provide the excitement and inspiration for new creativity.

Always enthusiastic to broaden his field, the opportunity to work to commission provides another facet to the *First Glass* workshop. With commissioned glassware from private clients to large organisations and the availability of work through galleries and quality retail outlets, both in the UK and overseas, Robert's aim to bring glassware of a high standard of craftsmanship and design to the wider audience, has quickly become a reality.

A new workshop in the London area is planned to open in late 1992 / early 1993, where both glassmaking and the FIRST GLASS designs will be on show.

JEFF SOAN
Toymaker

Jeff spent several years on a remote Greek island, where he became involved in many projects culminating in a book recording the flora, fauna and fast-disappearing artefacts of Greek rural life. On his return he took a City and Guilds course in Toymaking at the London College of Furniture Makers.

He now produces a large range of wooden toys, but recently the main direction has been in the articulation of wood. By cutting it into small sections and securing it to canvas, the wood is given sinuous movement, and by burning the surface to enhance and raise the grain, the toys become disconcertingly life-like. His raw material is gathered from London's numerous rubbish skips, discarded furniture, and more recently wind-felled trees.

The range includes fish, snakes and pythons, octopus, lizards, crocodiles and mermaids.

Jeff became a member of the British Toymakers Guild in 1988, won the Polka prize in 1989, became 'Toymaker of the Year' in 1990. He is married with three children and lives in London, working from a spreading shed in the garden.

Pam Schomberg
GALLERY
12 St John's Street
COLCHESTER

PORTCULLIS

74 Russell Way, Metro Centre, Gateshead NE11 7XX 091 460 6345

Open 10am - 8pm Mon, Tues, Wed & Fri, 10am - 9pm Thurs, 9am - 7pm Sat. and every Bank Holiday.

Portcullis, one of the few Crafts Council registered galleries in the North of England, is a spacious gallery/shop set in the heart of the Metro Centre, Europe's largest shopping complex.

Portcullis is situated on the upper floor of the Metro Centre in the blue quadrant above the cinema. When arriving by car on the third floor of the blue multi-storey car park, this will bring you out directly opposite Portcullis.

Our brightly lit windows attract both serious collectors and interested shoppers alike, all of whom are welcome.

Portcullis was set up by Gateshead's Metropolitan Borough Council's Libraries and Arts Service as a self-financing unit in 1988 to promote arts and crafts from and in the region. The unit has now been open for four years and continues to grow from strength to strength.

We pride ourselves on our relaxed and informal atmosphere where people are encouraged to browse, comment and ask questions upon the work on sale. We try to answer all questions you may have, so do come in and ask!

Mediums on show are glass, ceramics, metalwork, wood, papiermache and textiles. Also on sale are both precious and non-precious jewellery.

All work is of top quality and can only be defined as 'can be functional or purely decorative, but always beautiful, original and exciting, well made and well designed'.

We encourage commissions to be taken up when a unique piece of work is required and Corporate gifts are often undertaken.

Portcullis aims to show arts and crafts to everyone in the region. We like to feel that the work is within everyone's reach, so we take part in a scheme run by Northern Arts, the 'Arts Purchase Plan', an interest-free credit agreement which makes buying artwork more available to many.

We look forward to your visit.

JANE CHARLES
Studio Glass

Born in 1961 in Edinburgh, Jane graduated form the North Staffordshire Polytechnic in 1983. Between 1984 and 1987, Jane worked in a number of glass studios including Stuart Crystal, Midlands; Strawberry Farm Glassworks, Jersey; and Anthony Stern Glass, London. In November 1987 Jane Charles Studio Glass was established.

Jane aims to combine skill and technique with strong design to produce exciting quality work which takes the shape of paperweights, vases and dishes. Over the last two years Jane has become involved in working with large companies like Nissan and British Coal Enterprise to produce quality awards and presentation pieces which are given to a wide range of people, thus allowing Jane's work to circulate in areas that might not be familiar with this type of work.

Inspiration comes from the sheer delight in physically working with molten glass. This, together with shapes, colours and moods in the natural world, means that the relationship between artist and glass will be a long lasting one that is hoped will result in the emancipation of studio glass.

STAN PIKE
Blacksmith

Stan Pike lives and works in the heart of the Roman wall countryside four miles north of Haltwhistle town, working from a building dating from the late 15th century.

Producing a wide range of ornamental ironwork and exporting to countries throughout the world, as far as Japan, he makes all his own tools when it is necessary, for individual commissions including gates, railings, door and fireside furniture, wind vanes, candelabra etc.

A large proportion of his work consists of three ranges of iron furniture for indoor and outdoor use, Laurel Leaf, Figure 8 and Gothic. All ranges can now be supplied fully upholstered.

Blacksmithing skills have not changed and are still practised today by a few smiths. These skills are used by Stan and even without the use of electricity, beautiful pieces of ironwork can still be produced. Fire welding, riveting, clasping, hot cutting and punching of the iron are just a few of the skills used.

Commission for individual pieces of work will be undertaken.

ANDREW HALL BA (Hons) MSD-C

Andrew established Andrew Hall Jewellery in 1988 after graduating from Newcastle upon Tyne Polytechnic with an Honours Degree in Three Dimensional Design.

He has his workshop in Maiden Law, near Durham City, where as well as producing work for selected galleries and shops throughout the U.K., he works to commission for private clients offering a full design and re-modelling service.

His unique range of silver and gold designer jewellery featuring textured surfaces has a strong sense of rhythm and movement often evolving into musical interpretations. In many pieces the polished and textured areas provide an interesting contrast which in turn emphasises the clarity and boldness of his designs. His work encompasses a full range of jewellery for both male and female; brooches to stick-pins, bangles to cuff-links.

In 1990 Andrew was elected to full membership of The Society of Designer Craftsmen.

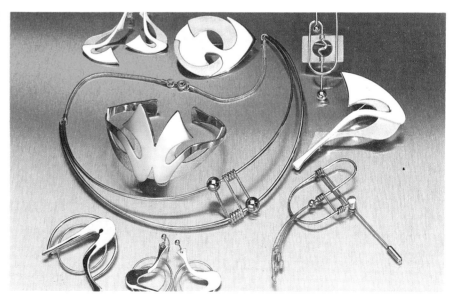

artists in wood

Paul Clare

Marvin Elliott

Mick & Liz O'Donnell

Dave Regester

Mike Scott

Hayley Smith

The Working Tree

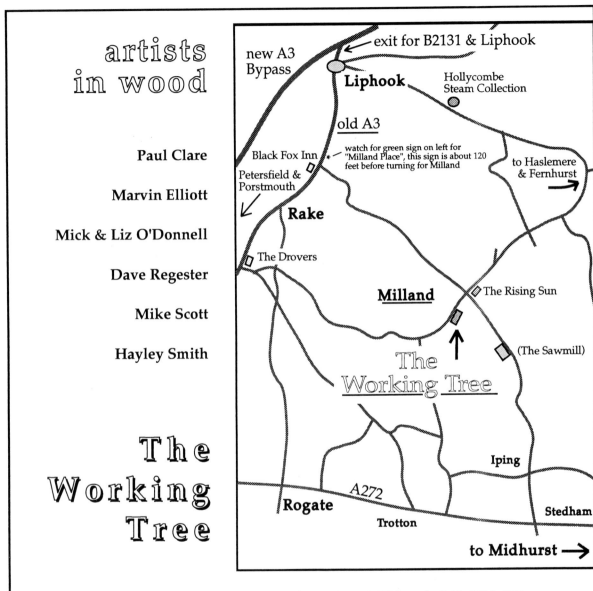

Milland, nr. Liphook, Hampshire GU30 7JS tel. 042 876 672
Monday thru Saturday 9:00 am till 5:00 pm

THE WORKING TREE

Milland, Liphook, Hampshire GU30 7JS (0428) 76672

Open Monday to Friday 8.30am - 5.30pm, Saturday 9am - 5pm

The Working Tree is the retail outlet for Milland Fine Timber, a company that has been campaigning for a radically different approach to tropical timber harvesting over the last several years. As such the shop and gallery reflect Milland's values: all the wide range of wooden goods and applied art (principally woodturning) are vetted for the correct sourcing of the timber used in making the item. Even the building itself shows a high degree of environmental concern, with toxic preservatives avoided in favour of durable hardwoods, very thorough insulation, a wood-burning boiler for the heating and elm weatherboarding to help this new and modern structure blend into its rural setting.

Jonathon Porrit, the leading environmentalist, officially opened The Working Tree in May 1992, owing principally to the fact that Milland Fine Timber have been major purchasers of sustainably managed tropical timbers imported by the Ecological Trading Co. since its inception in 1989. Milland are very much involved with discussion processes taking place internationally amongst the environmentalist community about proper forest stewardship.

The shop and gallery is an unusual place, and visually quite stimulating. The interior fittings of the shop were designed by Johnny Grey, the developer of the unfitted kitchen concept. Details of innovative design abound, noticeable as soon as you walk through the beautiful oak and ash front doors — also designed by Johnny Grey.

Lesser known species of responsibly harvested tropical timbers as well as native timbers are used in furnishings throughout the interior; and there are unusual racks filled with planed boards of hardwood for you to select your own material for that shelf or cabinetmaking project at home.

The Director of the company, Don Dennis, is a woodturner himself, and started a group called the Green Turners in 1989, a group concerned about the plight of the rainforests, and who were makers who took a responsible approach to the sourcing of their timber. The turners who display in the shop are principally drawn from that group.

Each of these turners work in native timbers, and have an international reputation for their work.

Turners represented at The Working Tree include Mick & Liz O'Donnell, Paul Clare, Dave Regester, Mike Scott and Hayley Smith. Marvin Elliott is a sculptor based in Arun who makes large animal sculptures out of reclaimed plywood.

Mike Scott's work is featured heavily, there being several major pieces of his large burr oak and elm bowls and wall-hangings displayed in the shop, as well as many of Hayley Smith's lovely bracelets, all carefully handturned.

DAVE REGESTER

I have been a full-time professional woodturner since 1974. Before then I worked in a solicitor's office and then went to University where I gained a degree in English and Philosophy.

I produce utilitarian items such as salad bowls, platters, breadboards, cheeseboards, pestles and mortars and scoops, which I sell through high-class kitchenware shops and craft shops. I also make one-off pieces which I sell through galleries and exhibitions throughout the country.

I am a full member of the Devon and the Dorset Guilds of Craftsmen and in 1982 I received a Major Award from South West Arts.

I am on the list of demonstrators compiled by the Association of Woodturners of Great Britain and have demonstrated at their International Seminars at Loughborough. I have also demonstrated at many local woodturners' groups and have increasingly become involved in tuition.

I am a regular contributor to 'Woodturning' magazine and have been commissioned by Batsfords to write a manual of basic techniques and two more books on advanced spindle and bowl turning techniques.

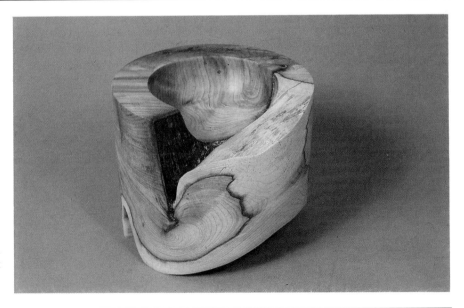

LIZ AND MICHAEL O'DONNELL

Liz and I started our woodturning business in 1974. All our work is turned green, primarily from wind blown local sycamore or sycamore which has been cut down for houses.

Being a relatively plain wood it lends itself to decoration which has been a direction we pursued over the last 10 years from which our work has evolved in three series. The 'Bird Series' was the first, being influenced by the coastal bird life around us. The second was the 'Nest Series' which came after a trip to Australia in 1989. The recent work is the 'Coloured Series' which have rounded bottoms, burnt edges and are completely coloured with stain so that the grain shows through. The 'Coloured Series — Mark II' are a variation on the theme. Although coloured, they retain the warmth and tactile qualities of the wood.

PAUL CLARE

I left school at the age of 15 and started a five year apprenticeship building London buses. After a City & Guilds Craftsman training I worked as a technician for three years, followed by a post as Tutor/Technician for Hornsey College of Art's 3D Workshops.

Four years later I started my own Antiques and Restoration business, which for ten years satisfied my need for developing a high degree of craftsmanship, but not much in the way of personal expression.

Then it happened! I saw some work by contemporary American woodturners and was immensely impressed, and after a period of enthusiastic development I became a full-time woodturner. I have been very fortunate that in such a short space of time (3 years) I have received acclaim in the Woodturning World and my work is sought after by museums, galleries and private collectors both in Britain and America.

All my pieces start off as rough chunks of wood chainsawn from a suitable log or burr from a sustainable source. I use native Welsh hard woods and some unusual American burrs and roots.

The rough piece of wood is then fixed to the lathe and worked with gouges until the wood suggests to me what form it would be suitable for and as I aim for original pieces, these are many and varied.

I enjoy experimental and innovative work drawing inspiration from tribal vessels, ancient pots and organic shapes, often employing surface texturing or sculpting or just leaving the beauty of the wood to speak for itself. Be it a huge Welsh Oak or Elm burr weighing 1 cwt or more or a paper thin translucent Holly bowl, all my work is finished with hand rubbed natural oils and my aim is to produce something of lasting value and beauty.

EXHIBITION OF WOOD

1. *Kevin Try (Dansel)*
2. *Simon Teed (Dansel)*
3. *Nicholas & Rita Hodges (Blakesley)*

THE DEVON GUILD OF CRAFTSMEN

Riverside Mill, Bovey Tracey,
Devon TQ13 9AF

*Open 7 days a week, 10am - 5.30pm
(Cafe 5pm). Closed winter Bank Holidays.
Admission to exhibition £1 adults,
75p students & O.A.P.s. Children free.*

At Riverside Mill the visitor can see and purchase some of the finest craftwork available in the South West. The complex, a Crafts Council Listed Gallery, houses a large shop stocking a wide variety of work, a gallery showing regularly changing exhibitions and the Granary Cafe where the visitor can choose from a delicious selection of home made food.

Bovey Tracey is an attractive small town on the edge of Dartmoor and Riverside Mill is a fine old stone building with a slate roof and working water wheel. This picturesque and peaceful setting is the perfect venue to browse amongst the pottery, wood, textiles, furniture, jewellery, toys and ironwork. Downstairs the shop sells work by Devon Guild members. Membership is selected, based on technical excellence, good design and individual flair. Many Guild members have gained national, even international reputations, a fact which is reflected in the quality of work on display.

The upstairs gallery hosts seven exhibitions a year and invites selected makers from all over the country to participate. The result is an exciting and varied selection of exhibitions.

The relaxed atmosphere of the centre is carried through to the Granary Cafe, where the visitor can sit and admire the pictures hung around the whitewashed interior or enjoy the sunshine in the attractive paved courtyard. The Cafe is featured in 'The Vegetarian Good.Food Guide' but also serves meat dishes.

ALAN CAIGER-SMITH

Alan Caiger-Smith started Aldermaston Pottery in 1955, converting the derelict village smithy into a studio-workshop. Since 1961 he has worked with a small team of assistants, mostly skilled potters in their own right, producing tin-glaze earthenware painted in a wide range of colours, and wood-fired lustre from copper and silver pigments. This kind of lustre should not be confused with the gold and platinum lustres used in industry, the effects are very different and the technique is too variable to be used in an industrial context.

Aldermaston Pottery produces a considerable range of work, from tableware to relatively ceremonial vessels, such as the 120 chalices used for the open-street communion in Oxford in 1987, and the enormous pots, four feet high, commissioned and recently completed for the new Pearl Assurance headquarters at Peterborough.

The Pottery is situated in the middle of Aldermaston village and is open to the public. They refine their own earthenware clay with a filter-press, and most of the pots are fired with waste wood from cricket-bat willows, which are grown commercially in the surrounding countryside.

Alan's pots have been exhibited in the USA, Canada, Japan, Australia and New Zealand, India, the United Arab Emirates, and in every country of Western Europe, and he is represented in the Victoria and Albert Museum Collection and in many public collections abroad.

Alan's publications include *Tin-Glaze Pottery* (Faber 1973), *Piccolpasso's Three Books of the Potter's Art 1558* (Scolar Press 1980), and *Lustre Pottery* (Faber 1985 and Herbert Press 1991).

POTTERY AS ART

In the beginning I think I was drawn to pottery partly because it is concerned not only with art but with things that play a part in life and are actually used and handled, either day by day or on special occasions, and are not just art-objects put aside on a pedestal. The basis of pottery is extremely simple — a vessel that holds something and that is itself holdable. I keep returning to this simple point of reference but it extends into infinitely subtle variations of form, colour, design and imagery. Behind them all, however, remains the simple requirement of holding and being holdable. Whatever decoration I use refers back to that.

When pots are not actually in use, they are put aside and seen and enjoyed, and this is where decoration and colour come in. What I aim for in decoration is not just an attractive embellishment. I think of it as a dance of colour and line and brushwork, rather as TS Eliot meant when he described a Chinese jar as 'moving perpetually in its own stillness'. The still form and the design belong completely together.

There are many kinds of decoration. On a plate it may be very simple line and colour, taking its place amongst many other things on a table. On a more 'important' vessel, a large bowl or vase or jar, it can be relatively complex, a system of colours and rhythms comparable to a painting, something that satisfies the eye and is a focus for feelings and associations. Decoration at its best can never grow stale; it is always life-enhancing and is always being seen in new ways, sometimes unexpectedly.

The challenge to me as a maker is to produce pots that serve a purpose and are something more besides. It's a very open-ended pursuit, and it continues to involve me in new ideas, new projects, and in technical experimentation, especially in the field of wood-fired lustre, where the colours are especially evocative.

Alan Caiger-Smith

PAUL CATON

Paul Caton was born in 1950, was brought up in Devon and had a Rudolf Steiner education in Sussex. The School put great emphasis on art, music and craft and this introduction influenced Paul's creative spirit. At 18 Paul joined the Swiss forestry service for three years working in the mountain high forest and lowland mixed woodlands. The Swiss experience provided a good understanding of trees and wood and he did several woodcarvings in his spare time. In 1971 he returned to England and began his career as a sculptor. Over the next five years he made dozens of sculpture for architects, interior designers and private commissions. The largest commission was for Okehampton town centre carved from 6½ tons of granite. He was in the Devon Guild of Craftsmen for several years and his sculptures were abstract forms and organic shapes that reflected aspects of nature.

In 1976 he carved his firs bowl and the personal satisfaction as well as the gallery and customer response was so positive that he specialised in the bowl form from then on. The great majority of bowls are carved from wood, but bowls are regularly cast in bronze as one-offs and limited editions, and occasionally bowls are carved in stone, especially carrerra marble. He was one of the first Crafts Council Index members and his work is in several private and public collections in Britain and abroad.

As sculptural items they have visual, tactile and aesthetic qualities that attract a positive sensory reaction. As utilitarian objects they range from small nut bowls to the larger fruit or salad bowls to the enormous bowl which children can play in or an adult can lounge in. Some bowls are finished with a carved texture, others are polished smooth, and some are inscribed with a carved dedication for a christening or wedding.

Paul has lived in the West Midlands since 1986 and enjoys teaching and demonstrating carving to children and adult groups in his workshop, at public shows or as structured courses at a centre or college. He fells trees for his own use from woodlands in Herefordshire and Shropshire and is always on the lookout for the more interesting hardwoods. He welcomes visitors by appointment and enjoys undertaking commissions of any sort. He is married, has four children, is involved with a forestry enterprise as a consultant, is a keen flyer and lives on a four acre smallholding in north Herefordshire.

A JOB WORTH DOING

Any job worth doing should be done well. Whether we are sweeping the road, building a bridge or indulging in art, the task requires mental, physical and spiritual application if the worker is to experience the satisfaction of a job well done and the public are to appreciate the total effort that has resulted in a positive contribution to society.

Work done that does not contain all three elements of this holistic attitude will lack, either blatantly or subtly, the completeness necessary for a satisfactory result. A strong but ugly bridge, a partially swept road or a meaningless sculpture cause us to shun these half-hearted efforts.

From the seed the tree grows, but in our case, in art, before the seed is thought, and before thought, inspiration. From somewhere comes a notion, a concept, an unstructured thought that sparks our imagination which, in turn, kindles the thought process, and creation has begun. This intuitive activity that defies logic is available to each and every one of us; it is timeless and limitless in its potential. It is also essential as the foundation for any activity that we judge meaningful to our lives.

It is frustrating but a fact that work done by the intuitive and inspired artist-craftsman often goes unnoticed for a generation or more. The public must be on the same level of receptiveness and appreciation to grasp the full meaning of a work of art. Sometimes of course, there is instant recognition, not on the facile level but at the deeper level when we are moved, when we recognise a truth or a reality is revealed.

This has always been the guiding principle of my work, to strive towards the goal that I believe in, and it is a personal creed to be not only aware of, but to explore more deeply the spiritual, intellectual and physical trio that are, to my mind, the essential ingredients of notable work.

Just as the plant cannot grow from sterile seed or in poor soil, so the mind and body cannot create unless the spirit is awakened. The spirit can be recognised as that still small voice within when prompted by the motivating will of the individual. The good seed and soil of our mind is formed by our true motivating desires that sometimes lay dormant in our sub-conscious.

In my work, I strive to emulate the Zen principles of silent power; to say little but convey volumes; to quietly move mountains, tingle the senses and stir the emotions. Though I am a novice, I recognise kindred spirits in Brancusi, Arp and Hans Coper. Work that conveys meaning and stimulates an interactive response along the path of growth, to me, is worthwhile work. Our lives are worthwhile if we consciously comprehend our present reality, live as one and at peace with ourselves, those with whom we share this world, and with the total environment in which we live.

Paul Caton

Wellspring Cottage
Deerfold
Lingen
Bucknell
Shropshire
SY7 0EE

INDEX OF CRAFTSPEOPLE

Many of the craftspeople contributing to this book can be seen at a wide variety of other galleries throughout the country. This index only shows which of our other participating galleries their work can be seen at. (Numbers in brackets indicate exhibition pages).